The Ultimate Gel Candle Book

The Ultimate Gel Candle Book

Marcianne Miller

with Julie Boisseau
and Alice Donnelly

LARK BOOKS

A Division of Sterling Publishing Co., Inc.
New York

*Dedicated to
Jessica Haley Parker
full of wonder*

PROJECT DESIGNERS
Julie Boisseau
Alice Donnelly

ART DIRECTOR
Tom Metcalf

COVER DESIGN
Barbara Zaretsky

PHOTOGRAPHY
Keith Wright

EDITORIAL ASSISTANCE
Delores Gosnell

ART ASSISTANCE
Shannon Yokeley

Library of Congress Cataloging-in-Publication Data

Miller, Marcianne.
    The ultimate gel candle book / Marcianne Miller with Julie Boisseau and Alice Donnelly.
        p. cm.
    ISBN 1-57990-357-6 (pbk.)
    1. Candlemaking. I. Boisseau, Julie. II. Donnelly, Alice. III. Title.

TT896.5 .M56 2002
745.593'32—dc21

2002069468

10 9 8 7 6 5 4 3 2 1

First Edition

Published by Lark Books, a division of Sterling Publishing Co., Inc.
387 Park Avenue South, New York, N.Y. 10016

© 2003, Lark Books

Distributed in Canada by Sterling Publishing
c/o Canadian Manda Group, One Atlantic Ave., Suite 105
Toronto, Ontario, Canada M6K 3E7

Distributed in the U.K. by Guild of Master Craftsman Publications Ltd.
Castle Place, 166 High Street Lewes East Sussex, England BN7 1XU
Tel: (+ 44) 1273 477374 Fax: (+ 44) 1273 478606
Email: pubs@thegmcgroup.com, Web: www.gmcpublications.com

Distributed in Australia by Capricorn Link (Australia) Pty Ltd., P.O. Box 704,
Windsor, NSW 2756 Australia

If you have questions or comments about this book, please contact:
Lark Books
67 Broadway
Asheville, NC 28801
(828) 253-0467

Printed in China

ISBN 1-57990-357-6

TABLE OF CONTENTS

Gel Candlemaking *Basics*

They're beautiful to look at, lovely to smell, fun to make, easy to maintain, and long-burning—no wonder everybody's talking about gel candles! If you're a new crafter, you'll discover that making gel candles is one of the easiest and most speedy ways to satisfy your creative urges. If you're experienced using waxes such as paraffin, gel will open up a whole new world of candlemaking possibilities. No matter what your level of experience with gel candlemaking, you'll find it to be a fantastic outlet for your personal expression and creativity.

The Ultimate Gel Candle Book greets the growing number of new gel candlemakers with plenty of easy projects and lots of helpful tips. For the more experienced gel candlemaker, we've offered projects that expand the whole concept of gel candles. As some of our friends say, "These sure ain't candles like Grandma used to make." And for those of us who are proud to be Gel Candlemaking Grandmas, we say, come on and join the fun!

Gel Candles:
The New Craft in an Old Tradition

In the following pages you'll learn about the nature of gel and the simple steps you need to take to work safely with it. Although professional gel candlemakers will certainly be inspired by our projects, *The Ultimate Gel Candle Book* is written for crafters who make candles in their home kitchens. Thus we emphasize unique candles that can be made with simple household tools. You'll get expert advice on how to choose containers and embeds that bring out the beauty of the gel; how to cause or prevent bubbles; make different kinds of fantastic layered candles; and create party displays that will dazzle all your friends.

The 37 projects in the book are designed to maximize the beauty and adaptability of gel as an artistic medium, emphasizing what is unique about candlemaking's newest oil-based wax. As in any creative endeavor, we made a lot of mistakes before our vision of a particular candle became a reality, so be sure to read the project instructions all the way through to get all our tips.

Julie, Alice, and I hope that you have as much fun making gel candles as we did writing this book. Please take our ideas and make them your own.

GEL, THE AMAZING DO-IT-AGAIN CANDLE WAX

You can reheat, recolor, replenish, and recycle gel wax. Don't like that magenta-colored gel you just made? Reheat the gel, recolor it by adding blue dye, and re-pour a fabulous new purple shade. Got too many bubbles in your gel candle? Just reheat the entire container in a warm oven for several hours and watch the bubbles disappear. Tired of your candle's design even though you've only burned it for 200 hours and still have that much burning time left? Remove the gel and the embeds, recycle them into other candles, and remake the candle in the same container. Amazing!

Working with Gel

Gel candle wax is a specialized mineral oil (a by-product of the distillation of petroleum) that's been mixed with a chemical agent to thicken it to a gelatin-like consistency.

Here's the easiest way to remove gel from its container. With a sharp knife, slice through the gel and cut out chunk-size pieces. Then, dig right in with your bare hands, remove the chunks, and place them in the pan.

Knowing that the gel is oil tells you other things. If you get gel on a silk shirt, you might as well say goodbye to it. But most porous materials that come into contact with the gel—work clothes and dishtowels, for example—can be hand-laundered and line-dried safely with a grease-eating detergent. Our advice, however, is that it is always easier to avoid a gel spill than to clean one up, so be advised that in every step of gel candlemaking, neatness counts.

The secret to getting gel off nonporous surfaces is to wait until the gel has cooled and become solid, and then just peel it off. If you try to wipe up warm gel spills, you'll just smear the gel and make a mess. Ammonia, adhesive-tape removers, mineral spirits, and other grease-cutting cleansers work best.

Big globs of spilled gel are better than little globs. You can *see* big globs of gel, after all. But little globs—oh dear!—they can get in, onto, around, under, and inside just about anything! Always know ahead of time where you're going to set gel-covered utensils, such as your stirring spoons or ladles, and you'll save yourself a lot of cleanup time.

Candle gel wax looks like a rubbery iceberg.

When gel has cooled, it's easy to remove it from any nonporous surface.

Keep gel off your stovetop burners. Gel on burners is hard to see, but you'll know it's there the next time you use the stove and the burned gel sets off your smoke alarm! As you pour gel, it can run down the sides of the pan and end up on the burner when you return the pan to the stove. So be careful and use the gel-friendly pans we recommend. (See Gel Candlemaking Tools, pages 11to13.)

Gel oil should *never* go down the drain. If you want to discard it, do the same thing you would with bacon grease—let it solidify in a covered metal container, and discard it with your trash.

Making Gel Candles—Safety First

Because gel is made with oil, it's flammable—that's why it's used to make candles. Respect gel's flammable nature and you'll be safe.

Oil and water don't mix, so if you should overheat the gel and it catches fire, remember that water won't put out the fire. Think of a gel fire as a grease fire and you'll already know how to handle it—smother the fire with a pan lid to starve it of oxygen. Keep a big lid set out and ready to use—you don't want to have to scramble for it in a panic. You can also smother a small fire with baking soda, which now comes in a shaker-top container that is much easier to handle in a hurry than opening up the old-fashioned box. Of course, you should have a fire extinguisher in the kitchen at all times. Know how to use it and keep it within easy reach.

Liquid gel is not hot enough to ignite newspaper if you dropped hot gel onto it. But if you spill liquid gel on yourself, it *will* hurt! Hot gel will stick to your skin and hold its high temperature on you long enough to cause a significant burn. In other words, be careful! And use those kitchen mitts and potholders. If you should suffer a hot gel

Keep your fire safety equipment handy when you make any type of candle.

TIP *Use a measuring cup to fill your candle container with water. The amount of water is the amount of gel you'll need.*

burn, treat the burned area immediately by applying ice, and follow up with medical care, if necessary.

Because much of gel candle making requires good timing, being organized and prepared is one key to success in this craft. Always read project instructions all the way through so you know what tools you need and what steps you'll take before you start. Keep your work area well-ventilated, well-lit, and efficiently laid out so you don't have to fumble for knives, skewers, and other sharp utensils.

If you're new to gel candlemaking, you'll be amazed by how quickly a small amount of gel melts. Don't try to speed up an already speedy process by turning up the heat—the gel can reach its flashpoint more quickly than you expect. And don't even think about melting gel in the microwave. It doesn't work, it may injure you, and it will ruin your microwave. Never leave melting gel unattended. Our advice is to turn off the phone when you're making gel candles and enjoy the safety—and the rare pleasure—of doing one thing at a time.

KIDS AND PETS, WE LOVE YOU—STAY OUT!

When you're making gel candles, youngsters can distract you, which could result in an injury to them or you, or to both of you. Gel candles are especially attractive to young children, who are fascinated by the gel's transparency and 3-D effects. They may eagerly reach for a hot candle, unmindful of the possible dangers. Our policy is simple: Keep young children away from your gel candles.

And, unless you want cat paw prints and dog hair in your candles—not to mention the possibility of being tripped while carrying a pan of hot gel—keep all furry folks out of your working area.

How to Burn Gel Candles Safely

Many people prefer candles made from gel because they burn so long, at least 13 hours per ounce of gel. For example, a gel candle about the size of a coffee mug can burn for more than 100 hours; a tiny tea candle would burn for 20 hours. Of course, you wouldn't burn a candle straight through its burn life. If a gel candle is allowed to burn for too long, it can get very, *very* hot, and possibly burst into flame. You should burn your candle for only about 2 hours at any one time. Then trim the wick before you light it again.

Gel candles also burn hotter than paraffin candles. They have pool temperatures (the pool is the circle of melted gel around the wick) ranging from 245°F to 280°F (118°C to 137°C), compared to paraffin wax pool temperatures of around 180°F (82°C). Although they burn longer and hotter, gel candles have smaller flames, which means it's easy to forget you've got a gel candle burning—not a good idea!

Don't expect other people to remember what you tell them about how to burn their candles safely. When you give gel candles as gifts, include written safety tips. (People love instructions with handmade gifts.) You have our permission to reproduce the following tips.

HOW TO BURN YOUR GEL CANDLE SAFELY

Don't leave a burning candle unattended.

Don't burn gel candles for longer than 2 hours at any one time.

Don't burn the candle all the way down to bottom of the container. Leave at least 1 inch (2.5 cm) of gel in the bottom.

Keep the wicks short! The longer the wick, the higher and hotter the flame—and the more likely the gel will ignite.

Before you burn a candle for the first time, trim the wick to ¼ inch (6 mm) high.

Every time you light a candle after the first time, trim the wick to ¼ inch (6 mm). That's right—really short!

Place candles on flat, nonporous, heat-resistant surfaces.

Keep candles out of the reach of children and pets. If you suspect a child has eaten a gel candle, call your Poison Control Center immediately.

Buying Gel

Craft stores usually sell candle gel wax in solid form, in small tubs that hold from 7 to 23 ounces (.2 to .6 L.) Order larger amounts through the stores, contact the distributors directly, or use the Internet. Just type in "gel candles" on your search engine and you'll find on the web an amazing number of gel candle resources, including all kinds of supplies, containers, and embeds—even newsletters for virtual neighborhoods of gel candlemakers. Visit our Lark Books web site (www.larkbooks.com), click on "gel candles," and find a list of some of the gel candle suppliers we know and trust.

Gel comes in different grades. Some high-volume professional candlemakers prefer a High Polymer (HP) grade, which stays solid during long-distance shipping, but is also expensive and not that easy to work with. Like most home crafters, we prefer the Medium Polymer (MP) grade, and we've used it in all the projects in this book.

Gel should be crystal clear, proudly showing off its lovely translucency. If the gel is cloudy or yellowish, it's experienced some kind of chemical reaction over time. Don't use it if you want clear, bubble-free candles.

Gel Candlemaking Tools

Unlike paraffin, which is melted in a double boiler, gel needs containers that can handle its much higher heating temperatures. Our preference is to heat gel in an *electric slow cooker with an adjustable temperature control* that allows you to dial a specific temperature.

An electric cooker with a specific temperature control gauge makes it easy to heat gel to a certain temperature. Thus you always know when it's the right time to put in additives such as dye, gel, glitter, and fragrance, and whether the gel is at the right pouring temperature for your candle design's requirements.

This handy appliance can maintain the specific temperature you want, making it safe and easy to melt gel away from the stovetop. (Ordinary slow cookers or crockpots, as they're called, don't have specific temperature control.) The slow cookers with the specific temperature control can be found in specialty stores and on the Internet, and are well worth the effort it may take to find them.

For stovetop heating containers, any sturdy clean pan will do. The ideal pan has a *heat-resistant handle* and a *pour spout* on the rim that makes it easier to pour the gel into the containers and helps prevent spilled gel. You'll discover soon, especially if you're making candles with a lot of different colored dyes, that you'll be happier with several pans than with just one that you have to clean out after each use. (If you use glass heating containers, you can always see the color of the gel in the pan.) To clean the pan, just scrub it with a grease-dissolving dish detergent.

When you use a pan to heat gel, you need also to use a *clip-on pan thermometer.* You can't tell how hot gel is just by looking at it. The only way to know the temperature of heated gel in the pan is to let the thermometer tell you. The clip-on thermometers are inexpensive, and you can find them easily wherever candymaking supplies are sold.

How we ever made gel candles before without a *heat gun* is a mystery to us. We use it all the time now. Is the top of your candle a little messy? Just move the heat gun quickly over it to melt the gel a bit and smooth it out. Did air bubbles have a population explosion against the inside walls of your glass containers? Warm

Here are the ideal stovetop heating tools: a pan with a heat-resistant handle and pouring spout, a clip-on thermometer, and a ladle to control pouring.

After a short burn, these containers shattered. Too late we realized that the glass—thick at the bottom—was actually thin at the top. The lesson? Double check the thickness of your containers from top to bottom. And unless the glass is *very* thick, don't use containers that are less than 2 to 3 inches (5 to 7.6 cm) in diameter.

up the glass with the heat gun and sometimes that small amount of heat can completely fix the problem. You can find heat guns at your local craft store or home improvement center. Always follow the manufacturer's instructions.

Even if you have a pour spout on your pan, sometimes you need more control in your pouring and that's where *ladles* really help. Two ladles, one large, one small, should handle most of the pouring jobs you'll have.

Use *metal spoons* and *metal skewers* when stirring gel or inserting embeds. Wood utensils can react chemically with the gel and cause it to bubble excessively, so don't use them.

Cookie sheets are ideal to make large layers of colored gel for cutouts, and to hold candles when reheating them in the oven. Small glass *baking dishes* are useful for making small, thick layers of gel to cut into chunks.

Utility knives, paring knives, pizza cutters, cutting boards, hot-glue guns, tweezers, pliers, wire cutters, clothes pins, bamboo skewers, metal skewers, scissors, a tape measure, masking tape—these are the smaller tools every gel candlemaker needs. It's a good idea to gather all your tools and reserve them just for candlemaking, so you won't have to interrupt your creative urges by rummaging through the junk drawer.

Except for the heat gun, you probably already have in your kitchen all the tools you need to make beautiful gel candles.

Heating Gel

Although the term "melt" is commonly used among gel candlemakers (including in this book), the truth is gel doesn't really melt. It simply decreases in viscosity—or *liquefies*—as it is heated. Conversely, as the liquid gel is cooled, it increases in viscosity—or solidifies to its hardened, gel state. Unlike paraffin, which has a definite melting point, gel's liquefication/solidification process takes place gradually, over a range of temperatures.

Heating gel is a process of achieving the right temperature range for what you want the gel to do. For example, you must first heat gel at a high enough temperature to liquefy it. But if you add items such as dye or fragrance—which require time to stir thoroughly—the gel loses some heat. So you may need to reheat the gel to your desired pouring temperature. Depending on how much gel you are heating, what you put into it, and how high you want the pouring temperature to be (which relates to how many bubbles you want), the time it takes to reach a temperature range can be anywhere from a few seconds to many minutes.

Paraffin wax tools are simple: Use a double boiler or a metal pitcher placed in a pan of hot water to melt the wax. A grater shaves blocks of paraffin wax; a whisk whips melted wax.

Tools for Paraffin Wax

Sometimes you'll want to use paraffin wax as part of your candle's design. It's more efficient to have separate heating equipment for paraffin, since paraffin melts at a lower temperature than gel. Melt paraffin wax in the top of a double boiler, or in a pitcher placed in a pan of hot water, and stir it gently. Use the thermometer to guide you to paraffin's melting point—about 140°F (60°C).

To heat large batches of gel, cut the gel into chunks before placing them into the pan.

You don't need fancy glass or crystal to make beautiful gel candles. Gel transforms everyday glasses.

Gels produced by different manufacturers can vary. That's why, in all the instructions for the projects in this book, we refer you to the manufacturer's recommendations, which are included on the gel package, or are available from the manufacturer.

On the other hand, we realize that, for any number of unforeseen reasons, a very small minority of our readers might not have the manufacturer's recommendations. Rather than having a reader guess—and guess *wrong*—about gel's temperature ranges, we offer a range of temperatures as guidelines to help if you're in a pinch. (See the table to the right.) Be aware that temperatures in your particular candlemaking situation can vary considerably from these ranges.

Some candlemakers may have experimented with temperature ranges to suit their specific situations—but what works for them may not work for you. Our advice is to err on the side of extreme caution, following manufacturer's recommendations.

The *"melting"* or *liquefication range*, when solid gel becomes liquid (the consistency of corn syrup) is 180°F to 220°F (82°C to 104°C).

The pouring range is 190°F to 205°F (88°C to 96°C).

If you want a lot of bubbles, pour at a temperature at the lower end of the range.

If you want fewer bubbles, pour at a temperature at the higher end of the range.

The baking or reheating range is 170°F to 175°F (77°C to 79°C).

The cooling range, when the liquid gel becomes solid, is 140°F to 167°F (60°C to 75°C).

Warning: Never heat gel as high as 230°F (110°C). It's unsafe—gel can start burning at this temperature. And it's wasteful. If you scorch the gel, it's ruined and there's no way to save it. You'll have to discard it.

Conquering Bubbles

There are five factors we know of that affect the amount of bubbling in your gel candles: 1) the temperature of the container; 2) the temperature of the gel when you pour it; 3) the pouring method you use; 4) the reaction of the gel to items you put into it, such as spoons, fragrances, and embeds; 5) the method you use to cool the gel. How successfully you handle each factor depends on the elements in the candle, your experience and skill—and luck!

Preheat Your Container

A warm container is less likely to cause bubbling. Warm up your container before you pour the gel into it by putting the container in a warm oven (175°F [80°C] or less) for about 10 minutes. It's easy to remember to do this. Just put the container in the oven right after you put the gel in the pan or slow cooker. (Don't forget to use protection on your hands when you remove and handle the hot container.) When you are trying to keep a container warm during a long process, such as making many layers, consider keeping it in a cool water bath. (See the Sunset Silhouette project on page 56.)

Check Your Pouring Temperature

Generally, the higher the pouring temperature, the fewer the bubbles. That means for each candle, and each pouring of each candle. When you're making more than one candle at a time, double-check the temperature before you pour each candle. And when you're pouring more than one layer, check each layer. Melted gel cools quickly. You might have a temperature at the high end of the pouring range when you pour your first candle, but in just a few minutes between pours, the gel temperature could drop 50°F (10°C) and produce twice as many bubbles in the later candles.

Too many bubbles can ruin the look of a gel candle.

Pouring gel is easy once you get the hang of it. Tilt your container even further to the side to help reduce bubbling.

Perfect Your Pouring Method

The way you pour the gel affects how much air gets into the gel, thereby affecting the quantity of bubbles. To minimize bubbles, pour the gel as you would pour a beer to get fewer suds—by holding the container at an angle.

Use Only Gel-Compatible Additives and Embeds

If an item is not compatible with gel—utensils, or embeds, or additives such as dye, glitter, or fragrance—it can cloud the gel, or ruin your design with too many bubbles, or worse, it can be dangerous. Especially with fragrances, gel compatibility is a big issue. Non-compatible fragrances can also lower the burning point, making the candle unsafe. See the sections on fragrances, pages 21 to 22 and embeds, pages 25 to 26.

Pre-Treat Your Embeds

People might think we're being picky, but our advice really is to spend the extra moments it takes to pre-treat items before using them as embeds. Pour a small amount of hot gel into a bowl, and coat the items in the gel. Watch for bubbles. If none appear, your embed is fine. Use tweezers to remove the items, holding them over the gel to let the excess gel drip back into the bowl.

If bubbles do appear, stir occasionally, leaving the embeds in the gel until the bubbling stops and each embed has a nice, protective coat of gel. If after a few minutes, the bubbling continues, it's best not to use the item. Don't make gel candles with gel that you've used to pre-treat items.

Even the perfect embed will cause bubbles if it has impurities, including water, on it. Wash and dry thoroughly any object that you want to embed.

Sometimes metal can cause bubbling, so always pre-treat your metal embeds.

Perfect Your Cooling Methods

Bubble Conquerors are divided into two opposing camps: the Fast Coolers and the Slow Coolers. On the theory that quick cooling arrests the formation of bubbles, the Fast Coolers place their gel candles into the refrigerator immediately after pouring. (Rest the candle on a bed of dishtowels or other heat resistant cushions so the hot container doesn't break a cold glass refrigerator shelf.) We're not crazy about this method. First, you can risk cracking the glass container from the quick change in temperature. And secondly, bubbles can appear later anyway when the candle returns to room temperature.

We're in the Slow Cooling camp, preferring to leave the candles undisturbed in a secure place for several hours. When we're particularly concerned about bubbles, we actively slow down the cooling process by wrapping the candles in towels or baking them in a warm (175°F or 80°C or less) oven for several hours, even overnight. (You can also slow-cool candles by leaving them outdoors on a warm sunny day, but cover them or you might attract bugs.)

Each candlemaker's environment, technique, additives, equipment, and patience level differs, so our final advice about cooling is to experiment. Find out what works best for you and for the types of candles you make and keep a notebook of your hits and misses.

Quickly cool a candle when you want to slow down color bleeding, such as with the swirl technique on page 93.

Reheating a candle can often reduce bubbling.

Reheating Gel Candles

If a gel candle develops bubbles, consider reheating it in the oven. Remember the obvious, though: You can't reheat layered candles or candles with floating embeds or candles with meltable embeds, such as wax embeds.

Remember that scents can affect gel's flashpoint, so if you're reheating a scented candle, keep the temperature low, and that will also keep the scent from burning off.

Place the candle on a cookie sheet. In the worst-case scenario, the candle container might shatter and the gel might spill. Make sure the oven rack is level so your gel surface doesn't harden lopsided.

Adding Color

It's amazing how easily gel accepts color. You'll see that we played with color quite a bit in the projects in this book. We dyed whole candles, made layers, used gel appliqués, even turned candles on their sides and poured dyed gel so we came up with vertical stripes. (See Incredible Vertical Stripes on page 48.)

There are excellent dyes made specifically for gel candles. You can also use dyes made for traditional paraffin candles, which give a more opaque look. Don't use food coloring—it's water-soluble and doesn't mix with oil.

Dye comes in two forms—liquid and solid—and a little bit of either goes a long way. To color gel, heat the gel until it's completely liquefied (see Temperature Ranges, page 15), then gently stir in small amounts of dye with a metal spoon until you have the color you want. With liquid dyes, add a few drops at a time. For solid dyes, use a food grater to scrape the dye into small pieces.

TIP

Dyed gel looks darker in the pan than it will in the candle, so if you're particular about the intensity of the color you want, test the color before pouring. Place a small amount of the tinted gel in a clear glass container or white ceramic saucer, or place a few drops on a sheet of heavy white paper. Allow the gel to solidify, and then see how you like the color. If the color appears too dark, simply dilute it by melting more clear gel in your pan. If the color appears too light, just add more dye.

Depending on how much dye you add, gel colors can range from delicate to intense.

Making Layers of Color

Making candles with different colored layers of gel is as easy as making a one-color candle—it just takes longer. A successful layering design depends on the combination of colors, the size of the layers, as well as the method of pouring.

All layers in gel candles will bleed their color a bit over time. The challenge becomes how to factor the bleeding into your design and use it to your advantage.

If you place red and green layers together, for example, they will eventually blend into a muddy brown color where they meet. On the other hand, red and blue layers poured right next to one another would blend eventually to form a nice purplish color between them. But they would look fine, and appear more distinct as well, if they were separated by a clear layer.

If you pour one layer over a previous layer that is still warm, the colors of both will definitely fade into one another. Sometimes this is the effect you want, to create layers that gently meld into one another.

To make distinct layers, let each layer cool completely between pourings.

On other occasions you may want your layers to be distinctly different. The trick here is to let the previous layer cool completely before you pour the next layer (See Cool Layers on page 54). Patience is the key here. A candle with several layers can take many hours to complete. To really impress your friends, make candles with vertical layers (see Incredible Vertical Stripes on page 48) or dramatic diagonal layers (see Diagonal Layers on page 66).

TIP

Experienced gel candlemakers always keep their leftover dyed gel. Use clear sealable bags or glass containers. Store in the refrigerator if possible. To keep dyed gel sheets for future use, cut them into convenient sizes and place them between pieces of waxed paper.

Making Appliqués

Gel appliqués are easy and fun to make. Pour gel into a small baking dish, or line a cookie sheet with aluminum foil, placing the shiny side of the foil face up. (The shiny side is smoother, so the gel won't stick to it.) Spray any cooking oil—or even lubricating oil, such as the oil you use to fix a squeaky door—onto the foil.

When the gel is cool, peel off the layer of gel and place it on a clean cutting board. Use a paring knife to make freehand cutouts, or make precise shapes with cookie cutters.

To make thicker appliqués that give more dimension than cutouts, make appliqués from muffin tins or molds designed for soap, candy, or paraffin candles. If you use plastic molds, pour the gel at the lower temperature range to avoid melting the mold. Use a ladle to control the flow of gel into the small molds.

If you don't need enough gel to fill a whole cookie sheet, make "trays" of foil on the cookie sheet. Cut a doubled layer of foil to the size tray you want, fold up the sides, and fold and pinch the corners together.

Gel-compatible fragrances are easy to find in craft stores or from mail order gel candle suppliers.

Adding Fragrance

Many people think that making gel candles is the excuse they need to enjoy the lovely fragrances of scented candles. Scents can be common favorites such as lemon, pine, or peppermint; or exotic such as Passion Flower and Sahara Nights. Like gel, fragrances contain chemicals; sometimes, as many as 50 different aroma chemicals can go into the composition of a fragrance. When chemicals mix, if they aren't compatible, they can react negatively to one another. In the case of gel, if a fragrance is not compatible with it, not only can the fragrance cloud the gel, but also it can make the candle unsafe. That's why the only kind of fragrance you should use in a gel candle is one that is gel-compatible.

HOW TO KNOW IF A FRAGRANCE IS GEL-COMPATIBLE

Check the Label

When you see the term non-polar on the label of a candle fragrance, you know that fragrance is fine for use in gel candles. Non-polar means that the fragrance is compatible with the hydrocarbons that make up the mineral oil gel.

Do a Compatibility Test

If your fragrance doesn't have a label indicating it's gel compatible, test it, especially before you make a batch of candles. A gel-compatible fragrance should be completely soluble in mineral oil. Mix one part fragrance with three parts mineral oil. If it separates out or makes the gel cloudy, don't use it. If the fragrance mixes in completely, with no cloudiness, then make a test candle. It can actually take a day or two for cloudiness to appear with a non-compatible fragrance. After two days, if it ends up being cloudy, then all you've lost is one candle. Many—but not all—of the fragrances used in paraffin candles can also be used in gel candles. Just test them first.

FRAGRANCES HAVE TWO AREAS OF COMPATIBILITY WITH GEL—SOLUBILITY AND FLASHPOINT.

Solubility refers to the ability of the fragrance to dissolve easily in the gel. A compatible fragrance is oil-soluble and melds beautifully with the gel, becoming invisible. But an incompatible fragrance can cloud the gel.

Flashpoint refers to the temperature at which a substance will burst into flame. Most fragrances have a flashpoint of 140°F (60°C). The preferred flashpoint for fragrances in gel candles, however, is no lower than 170°F (77°C), which means that adding fragrance to gel can cause the candle's flashpoint to go lower—and the gel can burst into flame at a lower temperature than it would without the fragrance.

Adding scents requires a delicate touch. Experts suggest that gel candles contain no more than 5 percent fragrance. (We prefer 3 to 4 percent so the fragrance is subtle and catchy rather than overwhelming.) Add the scent just before you pour the gel into the container so that the heat doesn't evaporate it immediately. Mix the fragrance gently but thoroughly into the gel. If the fragrance is not mixed throughout, it can cause the flame to burn unevenly or make the gel cloudy. If the fragrance is too strong, heat the gel on low to help release some of the scent, or add gel to dilute it.

Don't use perfume to scent gel candles. Perfume contains alcohol and won't mix well with the oil-based gel.

If your gel candle is burning on the surface, you've probably added too much scent. Remake the candle, adding gel if necessary, to dilute the amount of fragrance in the gel.

If you have an allergic reaction to gel candles, it's probably not the gel that's causing it. Most likely you're allergic to the scent you added to the candle. Just make scent-free candles.

Adding Glitter

Sometimes all a candle needs is a little glitter to give it that extra touch of pizzazz. There are lots of glitters made especially for gel—they're easy and fun to work with and you can be assured they will be safe. Not all glitters are gel-compatible. Craft glitter and mica, for example, can be flammable and have adverse chemical reactions with gel. Always check the glitter label and follow the manufacturer's directions. Add glitter to the gel after you've added the dye and just before pouring.

Glitter makes every candle festive.

Gel Candle Containers

Unlike traditional candles, in which the container is just something that holds the candles, gel candle containers share equal billing with the gel. In fact, many crafters love making gel candles because they feel that all they need is a fascinating container. They don't need to learn any techniques more advanced than adding dyed gel and a wick. Potential gel candle containers are all around you at home: drinking glasses, jelly jars, glass mugs, and orphaned or outdated goblets. Flea markets and tag sales are great places to find vintage glass and oddball containers that make totally wonderful gel candles.

In general, choose glassware that is designed to be stable so it won't tip over easily. Very thin glass won't handle the heat of the gel. Thick glass containers are sturdy, and because they slow down the cooling process, often help prevent bubbling. The top of a gel candle container should not be narrower than the bottom, and the top should be at least 2 to 3 inches (5 to 7.6 cm) wide. If you are planning to attach your wick at the bottom of your candle, then you'd want a container with an opening big enough to put your hand in it.

Let's be realistic about tower candles. We love making them and we certainly love people telling us how impressed they are when they see them. You just have to remember that most of the gel in tall candles never gets burned because you can't reach down far enough inside the container to cut the wick. If you love tall candles like we do—just for the pure pleasure of looking at them—go for it. Gel burns so slowly that you'll get many hours of enjoyment out of the candle before you refresh it with new gel and a wick or melt and reuse the old gel.

Glass containers that are already decorated, such as vintage drinking glasses, make super-easy gel candles.

Just add clear gel and a wick to a colored glass container and you have a great-looking candle.

In the nesting technique, place one container inside another one to separate the burning candle from embeds.

Gel Candle Embeds

Embeds are the objects that are placed into the gel and can be seen through the glass container. Many gel candlemakers find their greatest thrill in gathering and arranging embeds that are unique, or have deep personal meaning. Found treasure embeds are everywhere—in drawers of old jewelry, flea markets, and antique shop bargain bins. In addition, the gel candle supply market is full of brand new embeds, made just for gel candles. New or old, the most important quality of an embed is its safety inside a gel candle.

Non-flammable Embeds

Once you start collecting things to embed in gel candles, you'll realize that the number of safe embeds is practically endless. Safe embeds are made of glass, ceramic, metal, and non-organic natural items such as stone, crystals, shells, and sand.

Flammable Embeds

Objects made with organic materials, such as paper, wood, silk, fabric, and dried herbs, leaves, and flowers should not be used as embeds. Even though you may not think of plastic and rubber as flammable, they certainly are at high temperatures, and they should not be used as embeds either. This doesn't mean you can't use flammable objects at all in your candle designs. With the nesting technique—one container within another—you can keep flammable objects completely separate from the hot gel. See Nesting Seasons on page 44 and Sweethearts on page 73.

Polymer Clay Embeds

Embeds made of polymer clay are becoming enormously popular among gel candlemakers because the clay can be easily formed into any shape you want. (See Spider in a Web project on page 36.) Although polymer clay is not flammable, it can get charred in very hot gel, so keep polymer clay embeds away from the wick.

TIP

If your candle is smoking or emitting an unpleasant odor, your embed may be the culprit. Stop burning the candle and remake it with a gel-compatible embed. If you know your embed is compatible, then consider other factors, such as your scent or glitter—are they gel-compatible?

Paraffin Wax Embeds

The trick with paraffin wax embeds is to first cover them with about an inch (2.5 cm) of cool gel to give them a protective coating; then let that gel cool completely and fill the rest of the container with hotter gel. Place paraffin embeds close to the walls of your container, as far away from the wick as possible.

POLYRESIN EMBEDS

Figurines made of polyresin have become extremely popular and some gel candlemakers have started using them in their candles. We don't advise this because the polyresin is flammable. If you insist on using polyresin figurines as embeds, then keep them at least 2 inches (5 cm) away from the wick—and never give such a candle as a gift to someone else. Even though you know you'll remember to keep the wick this distance from the embeds, you can't assume that the recipient of the candle will be as careful.

Placing Embeds

Tweezers and metal cooking skewers are helpful tools when you're working with embeds. Use them to place embeds in the container before you pour the gel and to reposition them, if necessary, after the gel has been poured.

If you want to position your embeds at specific heights in the container, suspend them with sewing thread tied to a bamboo skewer placed across the rim of the container. Then pour the gel gently so as not to disturb them. If your embed doesn't have a hook or hole for the thread, then use two or three lengths of thread to create a "hammock," and hang them that way. Pour the gel carefully, and after it has cooled, gently tug on the threads to remove them.

Use sewing thread to place embeds throughout a gel candle. Slip the thread through or around the embeds. Tape the threads to the sides of the container, or hang them from bamboo skewers. Carefully pour the gel. As it cools, gently pull out the threads, leaving the embeds in place. There will be tiny lines in the gel, but they're hardly noticeable.

Gel Candle Wicks

Wicks are the unsung heroines of gel candles. Their type, size, preparation, positioning, and maintenance are crucial to both the appearance and safety of gel candles.

Select the Proper Wick Type

Zinc-cored wicks are stiff and thus stay straight when they're inserted into the gel; they're the only wicks we recommend. These wicks come in several styles—with or without anchor tabs and with or without waxing. An anchor tab is a good safety feature because it helps prevent the wick from burning to the very bottom of the candle.

Select the Proper Wick Size

Refer to the wick manufacturer's instructions for guidance on what size wick to use. Here's a rule of thumb: small for containers with diameters of 2 to 3 inches (5 to 7.6 cm), medium for 3 to 4 inches (7.6 to 10 cm), and large for 4 to 5 inches (10 to 12.7 cm). Don't be tempted

to use a wider wick just because gel candles burn twice as slowly as paraffin candles. A wick that is too wide can cause the flame to burn too hot and ignite the gel.

Prepare the Wick for Gel

If you want bubble-free candles, pre-treat your wicks to cut down any bubbling they may cause. Coat the wicks in hot melted gel and leave them in the gel until the bubbling stops. Remove the wicks, wait at least 30 seconds, and then run your fingers down them to remove the excess gel. Pre-treat wax-coated wicks too, because the wax on them can cause bubbling.

Position the Wick Properly

If you want your wick attached from the bottom of the candle, use an anchor wick with a tab. You can attach the wick several ways. Weigh it down with a layer of marbles or sand; dip the end into hot gel and press it against the bottom of the container with a metal skewer; or use the handy sticky dots specially made to attach wicks. You can use a hot-glue gun—just be aware that the glue may react with the gel and cause some bubbling. With whatever method you use, loop the top end of the wick around a skewer and position it over the top of the container. After you pour the gel and it is almost cool, give the wick a gentle tug to remove any slack. When the gel is cool, unwrap the wick and trim it to ¼ inch (6 mm). Save the rest of the wick to use as short wicks for shallow candles.

Sticky dots make it easy to attach wicks to the bottom of your candle.

TIP

If your candle smokes while burning, your wick may be too large, or you may have used too much scent or a scent that's not compatible. Don't continue using a candle that smokes. Fix the problem.

Sometimes you want your wick inserted from the top of the candle after the gel is poured. Wait to insert the wick until the gel is almost cool (if it's too warm, the wick could just sink to the bottom of the candle—oops!). If you've waited too long and the gel is cooled completely, the wick will probably go in crooked. Instead first insert a length of wire or a metal skewer through the gel to make a narrow hole. Remove the wire, and, using the tunnel it left in the gel as a guide, insert the wick.

To give a finished look to your top-inserted wick, add a bead to the bottom of the wick (just bend the bottom of the wick back through the bead's hole). Insert it just after you pour the gel, and use the regular technique of wrapping the top over a bamboo skewer to keep it straight. This is also a good technique to use when you want to keep your wick away from certain kinds of embeds, such as polyresin figurines.

If the wick goes askew, you can just leave it alone and enjoy its wayward ways, or try to fix it by reheating it. (See page 18 as a reminder of what kinds of candles can be reheated.) If the wick is attached at the bottom and you haven't clipped it, you're in luck. Just wrap the wick around a bamboo skewer and reheat the candle in a 175°F (80°C) oven, keeping the wick taut. If you've already clipped the wick, exercise your patience. When the gel has begun to melt in the oven, carefully remove the container and hold the tip of the wick taut with pliers until it cools enough to hold the wick steady. If the wick is inserted from the top, remove the wick before you reheat the candle. After the gel has melted and started to cool, insert the wick again.

Use Enough Wicks

To burn smoothly, your gel candle needs a sufficient number of wicks for the amount of its burning surface. If there are too few wicks, the burning gel may form a tunnel, leaving the surrounding gel unburned, which eventually cuts off the oxygen the burning wick needs. As a general rule, use one wick every 3 to 4 inches (7.6 to 10 cm) of candle diameter.

Maintaining Your Gel Candles

The top of a gel candle is sticky, meaning it can attract bugs and dust. Between burnings, cover your candle with a lid of glass, cellophane, or clear plastic wrap.

Trimming the wick of your gel candle is not an option. You have to do it. A tall, exposed wick is a potential safety hazard because its large flame can generate enough heat to ignite the gel. Trim the wick to ¼ inch (6 mm) the first time you burn the candle. Then, every time you light the candle, make sure the wick is no taller than ¼ inch (6 mm). Keep it short; keep it safe.

To trim the wick, wait until the gel has cooled completely. Then turn the candle upside down, so no blackened bits of the wick will fall into the gel, and trim the wick with a pair of small scissors or nail clippers. Don't try to trim the wick while it's burning; the result will be a big mess.

Wrap the top of the wick around a skewer placed on top of the container. When the gel is almost cool, gently tug the wick to make it taut. If needed, use the heat gun to smooth the top.

Keep your candle out of direct sunlight and heat. It usually takes a minimum of 125°F (52°C) to begin to melt the gel, but in summer against a glass window, your candle could really start drooping. There are UV light inhibitors that you can add to the gel when you're heating it that can help your candle withstand the negative effects of sunlight. These additives are wonderful if you know your candle will be kept in the window.

Remove embers when they have been uncovered by the burning gel to create a level burning surface for the gel and also to make the candle look better. Touch embers only when the gel has cooled completely.

Above all else, if you tire of looking at your beautiful candle after a while, don't feel guilty. Just replenish it with fresh gel and a new wick, or remelt, recolor, redesign, and re-pour a brand new design. Have fun!

If you know you're going to burn your candles infrequently, consider making candles using containers with lids that can keep the candles clean when they're not being burned.

Stemware Spectacular

This glorious display cost only a few dollars because we found all our stemware at the bargain bin in an antique store. Champagne flutes, wine goblets, margarita glasses—they look spectacular together when filled with brightly colored gel.

BEFORE YOU START

Choose your glassware carefully. Avoid thin glass, and any pieces that have nicks or cracks, or wobbly bases. For large clusters, mix the shapes and sizes with abandon; for small clusters, be more selective how you combine sizes and shapes.

What You Need

Assortment of clear glass stemware

Candle gel wax

Gel dye, any colors you want

Pan

Clip-on thermometer

Wicks

SAFETY TIP

With this many candles, just as you would with such a large number of paraffin candles, burn them only outdoors or in a room with proper ventilation.

What You Do

1. Plan your dyeing and you'll save time. Some candlemakers like to start dark and add more clear gel to get the lighter colors. Others like to start light and add more dye to get the darker colors. It's up to you. Lighter colors show off the translucent quality of gel more and are perfect any time of year. Darker colors are more dramatic and are perfect for cold-weather events. Again, the choice is yours. We chose pastel shades such as pink, yellow, pale green, light blue, coral, and light orange. Have fun.

2. Do one color family at a time. In a pan placed over low heat, melt enough gel to fill the containers you've selected, heating the gel to the highest temperature recommended by the manufacturer. Use the thermometer to make sure the gel doesn't get too hot. Add dye to go a darker shade; add gel to go lighter. Pour the gel into the containers. Save any leftover dyed gel for other containers.

3. When the gel has cooled slightly, insert wicks from the top.

4. Repeat steps 1 to 3 for all the different colors you want.

Roman Ruins

Small pottery vases, glass "jewels," and other miniature treasures evoke images of an ancient Roman villa sunken under the sea. On a base of white sand, this candle looks equally attractive unlit during the day or lit at night. Setting it on a pedestal accentuates the ancient feel.

What You Need

Large shallow container with slightly flared sides

Paper to work out your design (optional)

White sand (or beige mixed with white)

Gold leaf

Metal skewer

Silver glitter

Found treasures such as:

  Crystals

  Beads

  Pottery pieces

  Shells

  Jewelry

  Glass "jewels"

Candle gel wax

Pan

Clip-on thermometer

Wicks

For the Cameo

Clear glass pebble, flat on one side, curved on the other, about ½ inch (1.3 cm) in diameter

Image of a face on paper

Scissors

Decoupage glue

What You Do

1. Pre-treat all the pieces in hot gel to minimize bubbling. Wipe off the excess gel.

2. Follow the directions on page 34 to make the cameo of the face of the Roman statue.

3. On a piece of paper the same size as the container, work out the rough design of your pieces. If you are using a cameo, remember you can see it clearly only from one angle, so plan your design accordingly. Also plan where you'll eventually place your wicks, so they are part of the design.

4. Pour a flat layer of white or light-colored sand into the shallow glass container. Place gold leaf on the top and mix very gently with the metal skewer.

5. Sprinkle a small amount of silver glitter on top of the sand, but don't mix it in. It will give a shiny glimmer to the top of the sand.

6. Using your paper layout to guide you, place your pieces in the sand. Bury some of them. Let others stick up a bit at an attractive angle. You'll probably discover that you'll want to delete a few pieces, or add a few more, and do some re-arranging. Take your time.

7. In a pan placed over low heat, melt enough gel to fill the container, heating the gel to the highest temperature recommended by the manufacturer. Use the thermometer to make sure the gel doesn't get too hot.

8. Carefully pour the gel over the larger pieces and let the gel overflow gently onto the sand and the small pieces without disturbing them.

9. Let cool. Place the wicks where their light will be most attractive when viewing the candle.

DESIGN TIP

The many colors and shapes of the pieces in this design, placed against light sand, give it a playful look. Just because the bottom layer is sand doesn't mean you have to use an underwater theme. Experiment with colored sand and a variety of embeds. Work up different themes, using found treasures, such as "miniature toys," or "coins in a fountain." Try sophisticated abstract themes, such as all-white or light colored embeds on black sand—such a color combination doesn't photograph well, but it looks absolutely stunning in real life.

HOW TO MAKE A CAMEO

Cut out a face that is the size of a large clear stone with a flat base. Use a copier to enlarge or reduce the face as needed. Use the decoupage glue to secure the face onto the flat side of the stone so that it will be magnified when seen through the carved face of the stone. Smooth it with your fingers to make sure there are no air pockets. Use the same technique with photos of your family, to make a fantastic family tree candle.

Terrific Triangles

The triangular shape of these thick glass containers means they can be displayed any number of ways— spread out in a casual arrangement, massed into a circle, or arranged on tiers of different heights. The rich shades of colored gel glisten with turquoise glitter.

What You Need

Triangular glass containers

Wicks

Bamboo skewers

Gel wax

Pan

Clip-on thermometer

Dyes in your choice of color

Metal spoon

Turquoise ultra-fine glitter, or any gel-compatible glitter

What You Do

1. Attach a wick to the bottom of the container. Tie the top of the wick on the bamboo skewers.

2. In a pan placed over low heat, melt enough gel to fill one of the containers, heating the gel to the highest temperature recommended by the manufacturer. Use the thermometer to make sure the gel doesn't get too hot. Add the dye, stirring it with the metal spoon.

3. Add the glitter and stir. Turquoise glitter adds a quirky unexpected sheen of color to the gel.

4. Pour the gel into the container. Tug the wicks taut as the gel is cooling. When completely cool, clip the wicks.

5. Repeat steps 1 to 4 for all the candles.

Spider in a Web

Polymer clay embeds are easy to make, look terrific, and are perfectly safe in gel candles. In this stylish two-color design, a happy spider weaves her clever web on the inside of the candle.

What You Need to Make the Spider and Web

Oven

Tape measure

Polymer clay, black and white

Utility knife

Aluminum foil

Cookie sheet

What You Do

1. Preheat your oven, if necessary, to the baking temperature recommended by the polymer clay manufacturer.

2. Make the web first. With the tape measure, measure how wide the web should be so that it will fit snugly in between the walls of the container. Take white clay and play with it for several minutes to make it pliable. Roll it into a thin spaghetti-like shape on the aluminum foil. Use the utility knife to cut it into shorter lengths and arrange them as the spokes of the web. Make thinner lengths as the slightly curved webbing pieces and arrange them across the spokes.

3. Make the spider with the black clay, rolling it until it's pliable. Make two balls, one larger than the other for the body of the spider. Make black spaghetti strings, cut them into spider leg lengths, press them against the body of the spider, and bend them at an angle so the spider looks like it's walking. Place the spider on the web.

4. Keeping the whole design safely on the aluminum foil, lift it up carefully and set it on the cookie sheet. Bake it for the recommended length of time. When thoroughly baked, remove carefully from the oven.

What You Need to Make the Candle

Wick

Bamboo skewer

Polymer clay embed

Candle gel wax

Pan

Clip-on thermometer

What You Do

1. Attach the wick to the bottom of the container. Wrap it around the bamboo skewer to keep it straight during pouring.

2. Place the web with the spider carefully into the container, bending it gently like a real spider web, so both ends press lightly against the inside walls.

3. In a pan placed over low heat, melt enough gel to fill the container, heating the gel to the highest temperature recommended by the manufacturer. Use the thermometer to make sure the gel doesn't get too hot.

4. Gently pour the gel into the container. Don't pour directly onto the web, but pour around it and let it overflow, so that it covers the web without disturbing it. When the gel is cool, clip the wick.

SAFETY TIP

Keep your embeds at least 2 inches (5 cm) or more away from the wick. Although polymer clay is not flammable, the clay becomes pliable again as it heats up and may fall into the wick. If it does, it won't burn, but it will get charred and look really, really ugly.

Froggie Frolic

Yes, we know this is too cute and goofy, but we just had to do it anyway! You can't blame us—with its perky gel flower, the candle is so cheerful it burns off a rainy day mood any time of year.

What You Need

2 or more sturdy flowerpot holders
Clear glass pot that securely fits on the holders
Candle gel wax
Pan
Clip-on thermometer
Gel dyes, purple and yellow
Small baking dishes
Flower-shaped cookie cutter
Wick
Hot-glue gun and glue sticks

What You Do

1. In the small baking dishes, make purple and yellow layers of gel for the cutouts (see page 21 for instructions). Cool for one hour in the refrigerator.

2. Place the cooled gel layers on a clean cutting board. Cut out the purple flower shape with the cookie cutter. Cut a circle of yellow dye and press it to the center of the flower.

3. Lay the container face down on a flat surface; arrange the flower on the inside wall of the container.

4. In a pan placed over low heat, melt enough gel to fill the container, heating the gel to the lowest pouring temperature recommended by the manufacturer. Use the thermometer to make sure the gel doesn't get too hot. Pour a small amount of the gel over the flower to seal it.

5. When the gel has cooled completely, set the container right side up, reheat the gel to a high pouring temperature and fill the rest of the container.

6. When the gel is almost cool, insert the wick. When it's completely cool and the container is easy to handle, arrange it on the candleholders.

7. Glue the candle container to the holders for extra security.

Design by Julie Boisseau

Spark Plug Candle

One way to guarantee you'll make a candle that your man will actually like is to ask him what he wants. It was Julie's husband, Ron, a truck driver, who came up with the spark plug idea. Brilliant!

What You Need

Clear glass container (we used a shiny new Scotch tumbler)

Embeds: spark plugs, fuses, and taillight bulbs

Wick

Bamboo skewer

Candle gel wax

Pan

Clip-on thermometer

What You Do

1. Pre-treat your embeds in hot gel wax to reduce bubbling.

2. Attach the wick to the bottom of the container. Wrap the top of the wick around the bamboo skewer.

3. Arrange the embeds on the bottom of the candle around the wick so that some of the spark plugs stick up and give height to the display.

4. In a pan placed over low heat, melt enough gel to fill the container, heating the gel to the highest temperature recommended by the manufacturer. Use the thermometer to make sure the gel doesn't get too hot.

5. Let the gel cool completely, tugging on the wick to keep it straight, if necessary. When completely cooled, clip the wick.

Stars & Stripes

If your guests stand up and salute you when they see this fabulous candle, don't be surprised! Once you've learned how to make colors representing one country, you'll have even more fun decorating for an international gathering.

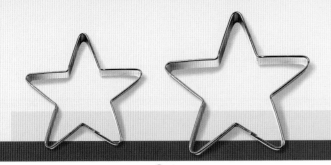

What You Need

**Clear glass oven baking dish,
  9 x 13 inches (22.9 x 33 cm)**

Gold metallic paint

Paintbrush

Ruler

Tape

**Single layer of stiff paper or thin
  cardboard***

Pan

Clip-on thermometer

Candle gel wax

Gel dye, red, white, and blue

Metal spoon

3 copper star cookie cutters

3 wicks

***You can use the back of a
  notepad. Corrugated
  cardboard is too thick
  and may leave debris in the gel.**

What You Do

1. Paint the rim of the dish and handles with the gold metallic paint. Let everything dry completely.

2. Measure the container into three sections lengthwise and mark them off with masking tape pressed gently on the handles of the baking dish. Cut two pieces of cardboard that will fit into the container lengthwise. Place the first piece of cardboard into the container and secure it temporarily with the tape.

3. In a pan placed over low heat, melt enough gel to fill the first layer, heating the gel to the highest temperature recommended by the manufacturer. Use the thermometer to make sure the gel doesn't get too hot. Add red dye, stirring with the metal spoon until it is a deep red color.

4. Pour the dyed gel into the section, filling it up about three-quarters of the way. Let it cool completely. Then remove the cardboard.

5. Position the second piece of cardboard so it evenly divides the second and third sections. Repeat steps 3 and 4. Instead of red dye, use white dye or lots of opalescent glitter to achieve a rich white shade. Remove the cardboard.

6. Repeat steps 3 and 4 using blue dye instead of the red dye.

7. Let all three layers cool completely, then arrange the cookie cutters on top of them. If your cutters are tall like ours were, press them carefully into the gel. If your cutters are short, just lay them on top of the layers.

8. Heat clear gel in the usual way and pour a layer over all three dyed sections. This smooths out any rough spots and gives a nice finish to the top. Let the top layer cool and set your wicks inside the stars.

Amethyst Mountains

Miniature mountains of amethyst and clear quartz rest on a sea of crystal-embedded gel.

What You Need

Round shallow bowl

Assortment of crystals with jagged edges and flat bottoms, enough to fit one edge of the bowl

Bag of amethyst chips

Candle gel wax

Gel dye, purple

Pan

Clip-on thermometer

What You Do

1. Carefully plan the layout of your crystals ahead of time. Look for crystals that have jagged, Alpine-like edges and flat bottoms, which are a little hard to find.

2. In a pan placed over low heat, melt enough gel to fill the shallow bowl container, heating the gel to the highest temperature recommended by the manufacturer. Use the thermometer to make sure the gel doesn't get too hot. Add a tiny amount of dye for a touch of purple. Carefully pour the gel into the bowl from behind the crystals so it will flow to the front and fill the bowl evenly and not "wash up" on the front of the crystals like an ocean wave.

3. When the gel has cooled slightly, sprinkle the amethyst chips on the gel along the base of the crystals.

4. When the gel has cooled, insert the wicks near the amethyst mountains so they can reflect off the facets of the crystals.

Design by Alice Donnelly

Vase in a Vase

You can't use a bud vase as a candle because it's too narrow to burn safely. But who said you couldn't put it inside a candle?

What You Need

1 narrow, thick clear glass bud vase

1 tall glass container, wide enough to offer at least 1 inch (2.5 cm) between its walls and the walls of the bud vase

2 or more bud vases of different heights (optional)

Candle gel wax

Gel dye, any colors

Pan

Clip-on thermometer

Metal spoon

Wick

What You Do

1. In a pan placed over low heat, melt enough gel to fill the bud vase, using the thermometer to make sure the gel doesn't get too hot. Add dye, stir it with the metal spoon, and pour the dyed gel into the bud vase.

2. When the bud vase has cooled completely, place it into the larger container.

3. Heat clear gel the usual way and pour it gently into the large container, letting it overflow and cover the top of the bud vase.

4. When the gel has cooled, insert a short wick into the top behind the bud vase.

5. If you wish, make two companion bud vases filled with dyed gel, but without wicks.

Nesting Seasons

Here's a lovely way to combine gel with pretty ingredients you'd otherwise have to avoid because they're flammable, such as dried leaves or silk flowers. The secret is that you don't actually embed the items in the gel—you keep them apart in separate containers, nesting but not touching.

What You Need

**Set of nesting containers
(shrimp cocktail servers are ideal)**

**Assorted ingredients for the
outer containers**

Pan

Clip-on thermometer

Candle gel wax

Wicks

DESIGN TIP

The wonderful thing about the nesting technique is that you can change the ingredients in the outer container as often as you'd like. If you're tired of a four season theme—just put in colored glass marbles, or fresh herbs, or flowers from the garden.

What You Do

1. Lay out your ingredients to achieve a pleasing combination of colors and shapes. We used the theme of the four seasons, but you can use any theme you want. We combined dried natural materials, such as the pinecones; and artificial flowers, such as the sunflowers, to represent the four aspects of our scene. You can use fresh natural ingredients, if you wish—just remember that you may need to put water in the outside container if you want them to remain fresh.

2. Make sure that the ingredients actually fit into the outside containers. Trim them, if necessary, and arrange them. Attach the wicks to the inside containers.

3. In a pan placed over low heat, melt enough gel to fill all the containers, heating the gel to the highest temperature recommended by the manufacturer. Use the thermometer to make sure the gel doesn't get too hot.

4. Pour the gel into the inside containers. Since the ingredients, in essence, upstage the candle, you don't have to worry if you get bubbles in the gel.

5. Place the candles carefully into the outside containers, making sure that they rest perfectly flat.

Gumball Machine Candle

Everyone at your party will be talking about this fantastic candle, so don't even think about trying to be modest about it. Keep the lid on during the daytime so people can see all the clever details of the candle. As it gets dark outside, take off the lid, light the candle and wow them all.

What You Need

Round "ivy bowl" glass container

Spray paints, red and silver

4-inch (10.2 cm) terra cotta pot

3-inch (7.6 cm) terra cotta saucer

1-inch (2.5 cm) wood bead

Small wooden flowerpot

Small hacksaw to cut the wooden flowerpot

Wick

Bamboo skewer

Opaque glass marbles, red, blue, black, white

Candle gel wax

Pan

Clip-on thermometer

Hot-glue gun and glue sticks

Silver ribbon (optional)

Keep the lid on the candle until you're ready to light it, especially if the candle is outside where unwelcome bugs might visit.

What You Do

1. Spray the outside and bottom of the terra cotta pot and saucer with the red paint. Let both pieces dry completely.

2. Spray the wood bead with the silver paint and let it dry.

3. With the hacksaw, carefully cut the wooden flowerpot in half lengthwise. Spray it silver and let dry.

4. Attach the wick to the bottom of the glass bowl and wrap it around the bamboo skewer placed on the top of the container.

5. Fill up the bottom third of the glass container with the marbles. Place them gently so you don't crack the glass.

6. In a pan placed over low heat, melt enough gel to fill the container, heating the gel to the highest temperature recommended by the manufacturer. Use the thermometer to make sure the gel doesn't get too hot. Pour the gel into the container. As the gel is cooling, roll the wick on the skewer to keep it taut and straight. When the gel has cooled completely, clip the wick.

7. When all the painted pieces are completely dry, and the candle container is completely cool, glue them together. Turn the painted red pot upside down so it is resting on its wide rim. With the hot-glue gun, attach the base of the glass candle container to what is now the narrow top of the upside-down pot. Place the small red saucer upside down and glue the silver knob onto it. If you wish, use a silver ribbon to pretty up the space between the pot and the glass bowl.

Incredible Vertical Stripes

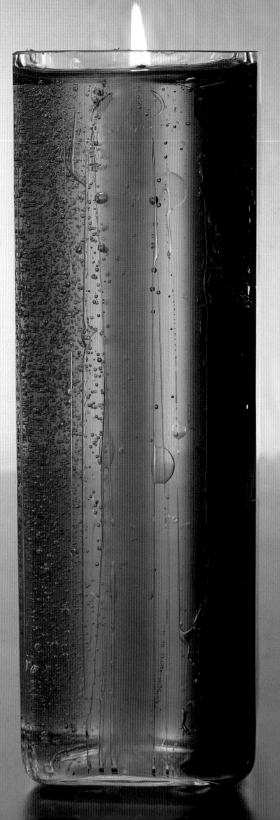

When Alice said she wanted to make a candle with up-and-down stripes, we thought she was kidding— and then when she showed it to us we were positively amazed. Her secret? A combination of careful sectioning, slow pouring, and patient cooling.

What You Need

Tall container with straight sides and flat bottom

Sheet of thick, clear acetate*

Tape measure or ruler

Masking tape

Scissors

Stepstool to raise the candle to eye level (optional)

Candle gel wax

Pan

Clip-on thermometer

Gel dye, any 3 colors

Metal spoon

Wick

* A full-page photo sleeve or overhead transparency works. It needs to be wide and long enough to make five sections to fit the width and height of the container.

What You Do

1. On the long side of the container, measure five equal sections from the top to bottom, marking them off with strips of the masking tape. These are the five vertical layers of the candle. You'll use these markers later as guides to help you get a nice, even pour.

2. Cut the acetate into four pieces. The width of each piece will be the same (slightly wider than the container). The heights will vary: each piece being one layer higher than the next, matching the layer marks you made in step 1.

3. Lay the container on its side and securely tape the shortest section of acetate over the mouth of the container, forming a firm edge. Place the container on the stepstool or other device (a level pile of old books is okay) so that you can easily check the level of each pour at eye level.

4. In a pan placed over low heat, melt enough gel to fill the container, heating the gel to the highest temperature recommended by the manufacturer. Use the thermometer to make sure the gel doesn't get too hot. Add dye, and stir with the metal spoon.

5. Pour the dyed gel layer over the acetate sheet to match the layer marks for the first section. Pour slowly so that you don't overflow the acetate sheet. Let this layer and all the others cool completely before you pour the next one so you create a sharp, distinct line between each layer.

6. When the gel has cooled completely, remove the first section of acetate. Tape the acetate for the second layer, creating a firm edge that will keep the gel from overflowing onto the previous layer. Heat and pour a clear layer of gel. (A clear layer between colored layers makes the colors pop out.)

7. Repeat steps 4 to 6 for the next two layers, alternating colored layers with clear.

8. By the time you reach the next to last layer, the gel has risen so that it's not easy to pour horizontally any longer. Turn the candle upright, and pour the last layer. Insert the wick into the center of the candle.

Decorative Dessert Candles

Make every day a dessert day with these sweet-looking candles made of gel and paraffin wax. Scents such as cherry, vanilla, and peppermint add to their charm.

What You
Need for All the Desserts

Glass containers or saucers appropriate
for each dessert

Candle gel wax

Pan

Clip-on thermometer

Gel dye, various colors

Metal spoon

Small baking dish

Knife or pizza cutter

Wicks

Paraffin

Double boiler, or pitcher in a pan of hot water

Paraffin dye, white and various fruit colors

Mixing bowl

Whisk

Metal ladle

Glass cherry for the sundae

Pie tin

What You Do for Gelatin Desserts

1. Make one color of gel candle at a time. In a pan placed over low heat, melt enough gel to fill one container, heating the gel to the highest temperature recommended by the manufacturer. Use the thermometer to make sure the gel doesn't get too hot. Add dye, stirring it with the metal spoon until it's smooth.

2. Pour the gel into the baking dish. Let it cool completely. Use the knife or pizza cutter to cut it into chunks about 1 inch (2.5 cm) square.

3. Attach the wick to the bottom of the container, making sure it is long enough to go through both the gelatin chunks and the whipped cream. Place the chunks of gel in the container up and around the wick, being careful not to disturb the wick.

4. Melt white paraffin in the top pot of a double boiler, or in a pitcher placed in a pan of hot water. (See instructions on how to melt paraffin on page 14.) When the paraffin has cooled slightly, put it in the mixing bowl. With the whisk, whip it into a whipped cream consistency and spoon it on top of the chunks of colored gel. Straighten the wick, if necessary, and clip it to length.

DESIGN TIP

Remember that paraffin burns more quickly than gel does. So if you burn off the paraffin and don't want to burn the gel chunks, just revive the candle by spooning out some whipped cream paraffin and inserting a new wick.

What You Do for Ice Cream Sundaes

1. Place the wick in the bottom of the container, making sure it is long enough to go through both the ice cream and the chocolate sauce.

2. Make the ice cream by melting white paraffin (see instructions on page 14) and scoop it into the sundae container. With the spoon, shape the paraffin around the wick to secure it. Tug on the wick, if necessary, to keep it straight. Let the paraffin cool.

3. Make the chocolate sauce. In a pan, melt a small amount of gel wax, using the thermometer so it doesn't get too hot. (Remember, a small amount of gel gets hot very quickly.) Add the coffee dye until the gel reaches a dark brown chocolate color, stirring with the metal spoon until it's smooth.

4. Using the ladle so you can carefully control the pour, drizzle the gel over the paraffin to make it look like melted fudge. While the sauce is still warm, top it with the glass cherry. When it's cool, clip the wick.

What You Do for Cheesecake

1. Make the crust first. With the light brown or honey-colored dye, color a small amount of gel till it reaches a light brown graham cracker crust color. Pour a layer ⅛ inch (3 mm) thick into the pie tin.

2. Now for the cheesecake. Melt the gel and add white dye and pour gel into the pie tin. When the gel has cooled completely, use the pizza cutter or knife to cut the gel into triangular shape slices. Place the pieces of cheesecake on the plates.

3. Make and dye enough paraffin to make the number of fruit pieces you want on your cake. (See page14 for instructions on melting paraffin.) We used red for cherries and blue for blueberries, but you can also make dark purple blueberries, or chunks of yellow pineapple and peach-colored apricots. When the paraffin is cool to the touch but still pliable, form it with your hands and fingers into round balls the size of cherries and berries. Place the fruit shapes on the cheesecake.

4. Melt clear gel for the fruit sauce and dye it. Using the ladle so you can carefully control the pour, drizzle the dyed gel over the paraffin fruit and onto the cheesecake. When the gel has cooled slightly, insert the wick.

Candles Fit for a Queen

What You Need

Glass urns in holders
Candle gel wax
Pan
Clip-on thermometer
Gold leaf
Metal skewer
Wicks

What You Do

1. Make one candle at a time. In a pan placed over low heat, melt enough gel to fill the container, heating the gel to the highest temperature recommended by the manufacturer. Use the thermometer to make sure the gel doesn't get too hot. Pour the gel into the container.

2. When the gel has cooled slightly, place a large pinch of gold leaf on top of the gel. With the metal skewer, stir the gold leaf slowly throughout the candle.

3. When it has cooled more, insert the wick.

4. Repeat steps 1 through 4 for the other candle.

DESIGN TIP

Make smaller gold leaf candles to accentuate the bigger ones. Champagne flute glasses and big wine goblets look especially gorgeous when decorated with gold leaf.

You'll feel like royalty with these elegant and oh-so-luxurious gel candles crowning your décor. Keep it a castle secret, however, about how easy these queen-size candles are to make with clear gel and gold leaf flakes.

Cool Layers

To get crisp, clearly distinct layers, cool each layer completely before pouring the next one. To make the colors in layers of dyed gel more vivid, place a layer of clear gel between them.

What You Need

Tall, clear glass container

Wick

Bamboo skewer

Candle gel wax

2 Pans

Clip-on thermometer

Gel dye, your choice of color

Metal spoon

BEFORE YOU START

1. Plan the number and height of your layers ahead of time. Beginning candlemakers might want to measure and mark the layers with tape on the sides of the container.

2. It helps to have two pans, one for the dyed gel, and the other for the clear gel—with two pans you don't have to clean out the pan after you pour each layer.

What You Do

1. Attach the wick to the bottom of the container and curl the top around the skewer, laying it across the top of the container.

2. In one of the pans placed over low heat, melt gel for the bottom layer, heating the gel to the highest temperature recommended by the manufacturer. Use the thermometer to make sure the gel doesn't get too hot. Add dye to get the color you want, stirring it with the metal spoon until it's smooth. Pour the gel into the container, carefully, so as not to disturb the wick.

3. Let the gel cool completely. Each layer must be cooled completely before pouring the next layer or they will melt into one another.

4. Once the colored layer is cooled completely, make the clear gel layer. Follow step 2, except don't add any dye.

5. When the clear layer is completely cooled, make the next layer. Continue alternating color layers with clear layers until you reach the top of the candle.

6. While the top layer is cooling, keep the wick taut. When the gel has cooled completely, clip the wick.

DESIGN TIP

To make layers that blend into one another, changing intensity from dark to light, all you do is adjust your color by adding clear gel to lighten it, or more dye to darken it. After you pour the first layer, by the time you make the next layer, the first one will be cool enough to pour the second one. And so on up the candle.

Sunset Silhouette

The secret of the graceful blending of the layers is to place the container in a water bath to cool the edges of each layer before pouring the next one.

What You Do

1. Make your silhouette. (See instructions below.) Press the silhouette to the inside of the container, making sure there are no air bubbles between it and the surface of the glass. The silhouette will adhere to the glass by itself.

2. Attach the wick to the bottom of the container and wrap the top around the bamboo skewer.

3. Prepare the water bath bowl, which is simply a bowl or pan that is big enough to safely hold the candle container. Fill it with about 2 inches (5 cm) of room temperature water. (Not cold water, because the gel-warmed glass might break.)

4. In a pan placed over low heat, melt enough gel to fill the container, heating the gel to the highest pouring temperature recommended by the manufacturer. Use the thermometer to make sure the gel doesn't get too hot. Add yellow dye and stir with the metal spoon.

5. Carefully place the container into the water bath for several minutes. This cools the outer edge of the layer of gel so it seals, but leaves the center of the layer still hot, so it will blend when you add the next layer. Be careful when you remove the container from the water. Wet bowls are slippery. Wipe off the sides with a towel each time you remove it.

DESIGN TIP

It's a lot easier to add silhouettes to flat-sided containers, but round containers give a realistic curve to images of natural things, such as flying birds.

What You Need

Glass container

Picture or profile you want to silhouette

Black polymer clay

Cutting board

Small utility knife or razor blade

Wick

Candle gel wax

Pan

Clip-on thermometer

Gel dye, yellow, orange, and red

Water bath bowl, bigger than the
  glass container

Towel

6. Repeat steps 4 and 5 for each subsequent layer, adding more water each time so it matches the level of the gel. Adjust the color of the gel, adding orange dye, then red to achieve the different gradations in color.

7. While the last layer is cooling, tug the wick taut. When it has completely cooled, clip the wick.

Making Silhouettes with Black Polymer Clay

Find a paper image with a strong outline. Roll out the polymer clay on the cutting board to a size slightly bigger than your image and approximately ⅛ inch (3 mm) thick. Place the image on the clay. With the utility knife, cut around the end of the image, making sure to cut all the way through both the paper and clay.

Fabulous Fish

Who can resist the 3-D effects of gel? No one! That's why underwater and aquarium themes have been perennial favorites of gel candlemakers.

What You Do

1. Attach your wick to the bottom of the container, letting the top of it curl over the bamboo skewer.

2. Pour a flat layer of sand and top it with a few seashells.

3. The glass fish embeds come with a floater ball attached on fishing line. Remove the balls and use the remaining fishing line. String all the fish on the fishing line at the lengths you want them to hang, then attach two of them to a bamboo skewer resting on top of the container to the front; and hang the other two fish to another skewer on the back of the candle. If there's not enough fishing line already on the fish, remove it, and use a length of new fishing line.

4. In a pan placed over low heat, melt enough gel to fill the entire container, heating the gel to the highest temperature recommended by the manufacturer. Use the thermometer to make sure the gel doesn't get too hot. Add blue dye to achieve a light sky blue color, stirring gently with the metal spoon. Pour the gel into the container, being especially careful when you're pouring over a large shell so that the gel overflows it gently and does not disturb the sand.

5. Tug on the wick to straighten it, if necessary. When the gel has cooled, clip the wick.

What You Need

Traditional goldfish bowl with flat sides

Wick

Bamboo skewers

Sand, color of your choice

Seashells, size appropriate for the container

Floating glass fish embeds

Fishing line

Pan

Clip-on pan thermometer

Candle gel wax

Gel dye, blue

Metal spoon

Choosing from among the many wonderful glass underwater embeds is half the fun of making the candles.

Sand & Surf

It's easy to create an intriguing side view of a beach, showing how it's kissed by both the ocean and the sky.

What You Need

Traditional goldfish bowl with flat sides

Wick

Bamboo skewer

Sand, white or beige

Glass palm tree

Seashells, size appropriate for the container

Pan

Clip-on pan thermometer

Candle gel wax

Gel dye, light blue and teal

Metal spoon

DESIGN TIP

Underwater themes seem to inspire grandiose ambitions. If you're new to gel, start small. Once you've gained experience, you can expand your aquarium themes to Jacques Cousteau proportions.

What You Do

1. Attach the wick to the bottom of the container and let the top curl over the bamboo skewer.

2. Tilt the bowl slightly and slowly pour a layer of the sand onto one part of the bottom of the bowl. Place the glass palm tree into the sand. Arrange a few seashells around it.

3. Heat gel in the usual way, add teal dye for the ocean, stirring gently with the metal spoon. Pour the gel slowly onto the bottom of the container where there is no sand, allowing it to rise up on the edge of the sand to meet it. The gel will set the sand immediately. Allow it to cool completely. Don't jog the container at all, or it could send unwanted sand into your ocean.

4. Heat a larger amount of gel to make the sky, dye it blue, and stir gently with the metal spoon. Pouring carefully so as not to disturb the sand, and fill the rest of the container with the gel.

5. While the gel is cooling, tug gently on the wick to keep it taut. When the gel is completely cooled, clip the wick.

Design by Alice Donnelly

Crackle Glass Urn

Pale colors of gel accentuate the delicate lines of crackle glass. All you do to create this candle of timeless elegance is find the candle urn and fill it with dyed gel.

What You Need

Crackle glass container

Wick

Bamboo skewer

Candle gel wax

Gel dye, any color

Pan

Clip-on thermometer

What You Do

1. Choose your crackle glass container carefully, since it is sometimes difficult to see nicks or chips in this kind of glass. The glass must be in perfect condition and somewhat thick to withstand the heat of the gel.

2. Attach the wick to the bottom of the container and curl the top over a bamboo skewer.

3. In a pan placed over low heat, melt enough gel to fill the container, heating the gel to the highest temperature recommended by the manufacturer. Use the thermometer to make sure the gel doesn't get too hot. Add a few drops of dye to lightly tint the gel. Turn off the heat but keep stirring the gel until it reaches the lowest pouring temperature. You don't have to worry about bubbles.

4. Pour the gel into the container. When the gel is cooled completely, clip the wick.

Hanging Agates

*Translucent slices of agate
float like jewels in candles of
clear gel.*

What You Need

Large rectangular vase

**Asortment of agates to fit the
size of your container**

Ruler

Tape

**Sheet of thick, clear acetate
(such as full-page photo sleeve
or overhead transparency)**

Stepstool

Candle gel wax

Pan

Clip-on thermometer

Wick

What You Do

1. Read the Incredible Vertical Stripes project on page 48.

2. Measure and mark the sides of the opening of the vase into three lengths of equal height.

3. Cut the acetate into two sections, one twice as high as the first. When the container is resting on its side, you'll tape the acetate sheets across the top of the container to hold in each layer of gel as you pour it.

4. Securely tape the shortest section of acetate over the mouth of the container, forming a firm edge. Place the container face down on the stepstool or other support so that you can easily check the level of each pour at eye level.

5. In a pan placed over low heat, melt enough gel to fill the container, heating the gel to the highest temperature recommended by the manufacturer. Use the thermometer to make sure the gel doesn't get too hot and pour gel slowly over the acetate to make a nice straight layer on the inside face of the container.

6. Let the gel cool completely and remove the acetate. Place the three agates on top of the cooled gel.

7. Securely tape the second piece of acetate, heat the gel and pour another clear layer over the agates. (If you tried to put the container upright and pour the layer, the hot gel could cause the agates to sink to the bottom.) Let it cool completely and then remove the acetate.

8. Stand the candle upright, heat the gel, and pour the last layer. When it's almost cool, insert the wick.

Solitary Agate Candle

Fill one-third of the container with clear gel. Hold the agate with clothespins on a line of wire suspended over the top of the container. Fill the remainder of the candle with the gel up to the bottom of the clothespins. When the gel has cooled, remove the clothespins and wire. Pour more gel to the top if needed. Insert the wick.

Pizza Dinner

"Come and get it!" Light up this clever pizza candle display on your buffet table and even your shyest guests will have something wonderful to talk about.

What You Need for the Whole Dinner

1 round glass pie pan for the pizza crust

1 small bowl for "grated" paraffin cheese

2 wine glasses for the wine

Appetizer plate to hold veggie cutouts

Candle gel wax

Paraffin wax, about 1-½ cups (.35 L)

Gel dyes, red, yellow, brown, green, black, and burgundy

Butter knife for spreading the pizza crust

Small flat baking dish to hold gel layers

Pizza cutter

Small paring knife

Heat gun

Wicks

What You Do to Make the Pizza

1. In a pan placed over low heat, heat enough gel to make the pizza crust. To give the gel a creamy shade, mix the gel with a small amount of paraffin wax (at a ratio of four to one). Add a little brown dye to reach the color of nicely browned crust. Heat the mixture until it reaches pouring consistency. (Since paraffin has a lower melting point, the mixture will melt faster.)

2. Carefully pour the mixture into the glass pie dish. Use the butter knife to spread it up the sides of the pie dish. Let it cool.

3. Heat enough gel to make tomato sauce. Add red dye to make a nice rich tomato color. Pour a portion of the red gel into the small flat baking dish to make tomatoes and let it cool. Pour the remainder over the pie crust. When the gel in the baking dish has cooled, use the pizza cutter or paring knife to cut the gel into 1-inch chunks. Place the chunks onto the sauce. Use the heat gun to melt down the chunks so their edges are smooth and look more like tomatoes. Set aside any extra chunks on the appetizer plate.

4. Crumble some of the paraffin cheese (see instructions below) over the tomato sauce and melt it down a bit with the heat gun to look like melted cheese.

5. Make the vegetable cutouts by dyeing the gel, pouring into a small baking dish, cooling, and cutting them out with the paring knife. Make peppers with green dye, olives with black dye, and mushrooms with brown dye. Arrange some pieces on top of the pizza and set others on the appetizer plate.

6. Heat gel to fill the wineglasses, adding burgundy dye for color. Pour into the glasses, and when the gel is cooled insert the wick from the top.

7. To slow down the melting process of the veggie gel cutouts, refrigerate the pizza candle before you are ready to light it.

8. Set out the appetizer plate holding the leftover veggies and let your guests add them to the pizza. They'll get a big kick out of helping you in the "candle kitchen."

Additional Items for the Parmesan Cheese

Double boiler to melt paraffin wax

Small glass mixing bowl to whip paraffin

Whisk

What You Do to Make the Parmesan Cheese

In a double boiler, melt a small amount of paraffin. Add yellow dye and a little red dye to achieve the cheese color. Pour it into a glass mixing bowl and use the whisk to whip the wax as it cools. Crumble the cooling wax between your fingers into small pieces. When it looks like grated cheese, place it into the small "cheese" bowl and insert the wick.

Diagonal Layers

Put red, white, and black in diagonal layers—wow! You'll get so many compliments on this center-stage candle, you'd better start rehearsing your bows.

What You Need

Large, clear, rectangular container that is wider at the top

Wick

Masking tape

Measuring tape

Diagonal support rack

Candle gel wax

Dyes: red liquid dye, white paraffin dye, black pigment dye

Pan

Clip-on thermometer

Metal spoon

Grater

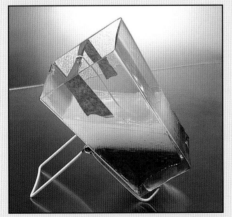

Tip the candle in only one direction to make the first two layers.

Three easy steps are all it takes to make this fantastic candle.

What You Do

1. Attach the wick to the bottom of the container. Run a line of the tape across the center of the top of the container and wrap the top of the wick around the tape to secure it, so the wick will stay centered during the process.

2. With the measuring tape, measure and mark the container with tape into three equal sections. Place the container on its diagonal support, such as the bookrack in the photo.

3. In a pan placed over low heat, melt enough gel to fill the first layer, heating the gel to the highest temperature recommended by the manufacturer. Use the thermometer to make sure the gel doesn't get too hot. Add the red dye and stir with the metal spoon.

4. Using the section marks you made on the container as a guide, pour the gel into the container, gently, so as not to disturb the wick. Let the red gel cool completely.

5. Heat the gel as usual, and dye it with grated white paraffin dye for startling white color. Keeping the container in the same position, and using your marks as a guide, pour in the white layer. Adjust your wick from the top if it has been disturbed. Again, let the gel cool completely.

6. Heat the gel as usual, and dye it black, using black pigment dye for a deep black. Place the container straight up and pour the black gel. As the gel is cooling, tug on the wick to keep it taut and straight, if necessary. When the gel has completely cooled, clip the wick.

7. A candle this big can burn for more than 400 hours. Be sure you keep the wick clipped short so the candle always look terrific.

Design by Julie Boisseau

Circles in a Square

Vintage turquoise candleholders and new purple glass bubbles make fantastic circular embeds in this square candle.

From the top, you can see how the candle was constructed.

What You Need

Square glass container with high straight sides

Assortment of round glass candlestick holders and other round embeds, enough to create the design

Candle gel wax

Pan

Clip-on thermometer

Wicks

What You Do

1. Lay out your embeds in the glass container to work out your design. We used five turquoise candleholders and seven lavender glass bubbles. To create height in the design, we turned two of the candleholders upside down and placed another holder on top of them. On top of the remaining candleholder we placed one of the lavender bubbles, and then arranged the remaining bubbles. In this way we used the same elements to create a different look when the candle is viewed from the sides

2. Place two of the four wicks directly into the top of the higher two-layered candlesticks. Attach the other two wicks to the bottom of the container.

3. In a pan placed over low heat, melt enough gel to fill the container, heating the gel to the highest temperature recommended by the manufacturer. Use the thermometer to make sure the gel doesn't get too hot. Gently pour the gel into the container.

4. Since the purple bubbles are filled with air, they tend to float. So if you are using a similar lightweight embed, pour a bottom layer of gel and allow it to cool to set the bubbles. Once the bubbles are set, pour more gel to the height you want the candle to be.

Fire Beads & Wire

Fire beads are fantastic in gel candles. The burning wick reflects off the many facets of each bead, making the entire candle shimmer in the flickering lights.

What You Need

Tall, clear glass container

Assortment of Czechoslovakian
   fire beads, or beads of your choice

Jewelry wire, 18-mm gauge, cut
   to length

Loom made of nails and scrap wood

Wire cutters

Needle-nose pliers

Copper wick rod (or pencil)

Wick

Candle gel wax

Pan

Clip-on thermometer

Metal skewer

What You Do

1. Cut the wire with the wire cutters. We used purple jewelry wire to go with the beads, but you can use any kind of wire that will suit your design.

2. Make your first wire shape on the loom (see photo below). Use the needle-nose pliers, if needed. Then twist wire around the wick rod (found in candle supply shops) to make a spiral. Add a bead and make another spiral. Repeat the pattern until you've made a spiral long enough for your candle.

3. Attach the wick on the bottom of the container.

4. Place the wire spiral into the candle, spreading it to touch the sides of the glass to help keep its spiral. A wide, loose spiral looks better than a tight spiral with many twists.

5. Curl the top of the wick over wick rods or a bamboo skewer placed on top of the container.

6. In a pan placed over low heat, melt enough gel to fill the container, heating the gel to the highest temperature recommended by the manufacturer. Use the thermometer to make sure the gel doesn't get too hot. Pour the gel into the container. If the wire spiral becomes dislodged at any point, push it back into place with the metal skewer.

7. While the candle is cooling, tug the wick taut. When cooled completely, clip the wick.

HOW TO MAKE A LOOM

Hammer finish nails into a piece of scrap wood in a formation that will give you the shape you want. The one in the photograph below helps you make a simple clover shape.

Vintage Stripes

What You Need

Assortment of striped glasses

Wicks

Bamboo skewers

Pan

Clip-on thermometer

Candle gel wax

Gel dyes, various colors

Metal spoon

What You Do

1. Attach the wicks to the bottoms of the glasses, curling their tops around the bamboo skewers.

2. Make one candle at a time. In a pan placed over low heat, melt enough gel to fill one of the containers, heating the gel to the highest temperature recommended by the manufacturer. Use the thermometer to make sure the gel doesn't get too hot. Add dye and stir with the metal spoon. (Clear gel looks fabulous, too.) Pour the gel into the container.

3. As each candle is cooling, tug on the wick a bit to keep it straight. When the gel has completely cooled, clip the wick.

DESIGN TIP

Stripes are common in vintage glass. Be sure your older glass is thick enough to withstand the heat of gel. And no matter how lovely a glass is, if it's cracked or chipped, don't use it as a candle container. Instead use it to hold straws or utensils.

All you need for a fabulously easy summertime display is an assortment of striped drinking glasses and different colors of gel dye.

Sweethearts

A flower-filled heart safely nests around the gel candle in the center.

What You Need

Glass heart-shaped bowl

Glass votive candleholder

Wick

Glass hearts

Assortment of silk flowers

Glitter

Bamboo skewer

Candle gel wax

Pan

Clip-on thermometer

What You Do

1. Attach the wick to bottom of the glass votive candleholder and place the candleholder on the bottom center of the heart-shaped bowl.

2. Arrange the glass hearts on the bottom of the heart container. Then position the silk flowers on top of them. Rosebuds are traditionally romantic flowers, but you can use any flower you like, to set any kind of mood.

3. Sprinkle the glitter over the flowers. The glitter won't burn because it's not in the holder with the wick, but it will shimmer beautifully in the flickering light of the lit candle.

4. Wrap the top of the wick around the skewer.

5. In a pan placed over low heat, melt enough gel to fill both the containers, heating the gel to the lowest pouring temperature (not the highest temperature) recommended by the manufacturer. Use the thermometer to make sure the gel doesn't get too hot.

6. Pour the gel into the central votive candleholder and then into the heart-shaped container so that all the flowers and glass beads are covered.

7. While the gel is cooling, tug the wick straight. When completely cooled, clip the wick.

Tuxedo Tonight

For a formal event that needs a sense of humor, make this totally terrific tuxedo candle.

What You Need

Tall clear glass container with a wide top

Tape measure or ruler

Scissors

Sheet of thick, clear acetate (such as full-page photo sleeve or overhead transparency)

Masking tape

Candle gel wax

Paraffin wax

Pan

Clip-on thermometer

Gel dyes, black, white

Wick

Buttons

Bow tie, sized to fit the candle

Hot-glue gun and glue sticks

What You Do

1. Measure the black sections and mark them with tape on the back of the container.

2. Measure and cut two sections of acetate the width of the black sections.

3. Tape the acetate securely over the top of the container on one side to create a barrier and lay the container on its side.

4. In a pan placed over low heat, melt enough gel for the black sections, heating the gel to the highest temperature recommended by the manufacturer. Use the thermometer to make sure the gel doesn't get too hot. Add black dye, and pour. Let it cool completely, then remove the acetate. Repeat for the other side.

5. Set the container upright. Remove all the tape markers.

6. Pour the bottom black section and let it cool completely.

7. To get the starched white shirt effect, add one part paraffin to four parts gel. Melt the mixture, add white dye, and pour to fill the center of the container. When cooled, insert the wick.

8. When the candle has cooled completely, glue on the buttons and the bow.

Fall Foliage

Inspired by the design of leaf veins in the bottom of the glass candy dishes, we duplicated them in the candle with inserts of shiny copper wire. The result is a celebration of fall foliage you'll be proud to display all year.

Use up any leftover gel by pouring it into small thick-glass votive candleholders.

What You Need

Assortment of leaf-shaped glasses

Paper, pencil and measuring tape (optional)

Thin copper wire (18 mm gauge), lengths cut to fit the design of your glass

Wire cutters

Candle gel wax

Pan

Clip-on pan thermometer

Gel dyes, various colors

Metal spoon

Wicks

What You Do

1. With your fingers, bend the copper wire to your design, cutting the ends with the wire cutters. Lay out the long vein first, then bend and shape the smaller side veins. Repeat for all the glass dishes.

2. Make one leaf candle at a time. In a pan placed over low heat, melt enough gel to fill one of the containers, heating the gel to the highest temperature recommended by the manufacturer. Use the thermometer to make sure the gel doesn't get too hot.

3. Add the dye to achieve the rich color you want and stir it with the metal spoon. We used burgundy, forest green, coral, and yellow.

4. Pour the gel into the container, about three fourths of the way to the top. Let the gel cool slightly, then gently press the wire insert onto the gel.

5. Repeat steps 2 to 4 for the remaining candles.

6. The wire is hard to see if covered by colored gel, so you'll add a layer of clear gel over the wire to show it off. When the dyed gel layers are completely cool, heat enough clear gel to pour a thin layer on each candle. When the top clear layers have cooled, insert the wicks.

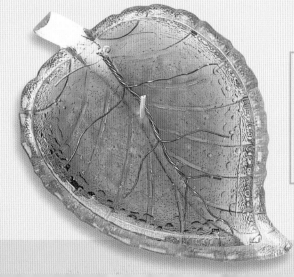

DESIGN TIP

Amber is one of those deep rich colors you can make yourself. It's easy. Just use three parts yellow to one part brown dye. Adjust the ratio of the dyes to get the shade of amber you want.

NOTE

Remember that a shallow candle can be burned only a short time, just a few hours. Replenish the candle by pouring a new layer of gel and inserting a new wick.

Fisherman's Catch

Let's face it. When you give a guy a candle he usually says "Gee, thanks, honey" and promptly forgets about it. So why not make him a humorous candle that he can put on a shelf in his private space and do nothing but enjoy looking at it? If you think he might really light it, add a scent he'll like, such as sandalwood or pine, and keep it low-key.

What You Do

1. Pre-treat the embeds in hot gel to reduce bubbling.

2. Attach the wick to the bottom of the inner container and place in the center of outer container. Arrange the weights, swivels, and hooks in a layer on the bottom of the outer container.

3. With the fishing line, tie the lures to wick rods or bamboo skewers at the heights you want them to hang against the sides of the outer container. Set the wick rods or bamboo skewers on the edge of the outside container rim, taping them to the edge of the glass, if necessary, to hold them in place.

4. In a pan placed over low heat, melt enough gel to fill both containers, heating the gel to the highest temperature recommended by the manufacturer. Use the thermometer to make sure the gel doesn't get too hot.

5. Pour the gel into the inner container, letting it over flow into the outer container so that the movement of the gel is slow and gentle and won't disturb the embeds. Keep pouring until the level of the gel in the outer container is at the height you want it to be.

6. Place another skewer or rod on top of the candle and carefully wrap the wick around it.

7. Let the gel cool completely, gently tugging on the wick to keep it straight, if necessary. When the gel is completely cool, clip the wick and trim the fishing line even with the level of the gel wax. The rest of the fishing line stays in the candle and you can barely see it, so don't worry about it.

BEFORE YOU START

Choose any fishing lures you like, including lures with feathers, which are flammable. Because the embeds are completely separated from the burning gel in a separate container, they won't be a safety hazard.

What You Need

2 nesting glass containers, about 3 inches (7.6 cm) high

Embeds: fishing lures, weights, swivels, hooks

Wick

Fishing line

Wick rods or bamboo skewers

Tape (optional)

Candle gel wax

Pan

Clip-on thermometer

Painted Ivy

One beautiful and satisfying way to create one-of-a-kind gel candles is to hand-paint the container. Not an artist, you protest? Nonsense! Many famous artists have proven that the more child-like your design is, the more impressive it becomes. Enjoy!

What You Need

Clear glass container

Glass craft paint in colors of your choice

Flat paintbrush, ¾ inch (1.9 cm) wide

Palette to mix paints

Oven (if you use glass paints that need to be baked)

Oven mitts or protective gloves

Wick

Candle gel wax

Pan

Clip-on thermometer

Bamboo skewer

DESIGN TIP

Double load your brush with paint. Dip one corner of the brush into one color and the other corner into the other color. Then gently wipe the brush back and forth on your palette to blend the two colors in the center of your brush. The result is a brush with three colors on it. Each stroke gives you instant highlights or shadows on everything you paint with it.

What You Do

1. Make a simple design that allows plenty of gel to show through. Paint what you know. Julie said she painted leaves for a very simple reason she knows how to paint them!

2. If needed, when your design is finished and the paint is dry, place your container in the oven and bake it according to paint manufacturer's instructions.

3. When the paint has finished baking, it will be nice and hard and look terrific. Use oven mitts or protective gloves to remove the container and place it on a safe sturdy surface.

4. When the container has completely cooled, attach the wick to the bottom.

5. In a pan placed over low heat, melt enough gel to fill the container, heating the gel to the highest temperature recommended by the manufacturer. Use the thermometer to make sure the gel doesn't get too hot.

6. Pour the gel into the container. (Don't worry about bubbles; the design will hide them.)

7. Wrap the wick around the bamboo skewer placed on the rim of the container.

8. When the gel has cooled, clip the wick.

Paints for Decorating Glass

Read the label on the paint container to make sure the paint can be used on glass. Also check if it's dishwasher safe. If not, plan to wash the container by hand.

Julie prefers to paint her glass containers with acrylic glass paint because she likes their thick look and ability to blend into one another well. There are also wonderful paints made specifically for painting on glass that give a transparent, stained glass look; they're more expensive than acrylics, but you don't have to bake them.

Martini Show-Off

These martinis, olives and all, look like the real thing. Candles with pointy bases aren't safe to burn because the gel gets too hot in the narrow space. We solved that problem in these martini glasses by making their bases flat, with two different and equally attractive techniques.

What You Need for Both Safe-Base Techniques

Martini glasses with pretty stems and solid feet

Acrylic water (found in floral craft stores) or clear glass marbles

Glass olive stir stick

Candle gel wax

Pan

Clip-on thermometer

Wick

Making an Acrylic Water Base Candle

1. Follow the directions on the package and pour the acrylic water into the bottom of the glass. Let it harden.

2. In a pan placed over low heat. Heating the gel to the highest temperature recommended by the manufacturer. Use the thermometer to make sure the gel doesn't get too hot. Pour the gel into the glass over the acrylic water.

3. When the gel has cooled slightly, add the glass olive. When it has cooled more, insert the wick.

DESIGN TIP

Since the acrylic water is permanent, all you have to do to make a new candle is refill the candle with new gel and a new wick.

Making a Marble Base Candle

1. Arrange a layer of clear marbles on the bottom of the martini glass and pack them tightly around the wick.

2. In a pan placed over low heat, melt enough gel to fill the martini glass, heating the gel to the highest temperature recommended by the manufacturer. Use the thermometer to make sure the gel doesn't get too hot. Pour the gel into the martini glass over the layer of marbles, being careful not to disturb the wick.

3. When the gel has cooled slightly, add the glass olive and the wick.

Sea Glass Sensation

The storm-tossed colors of sea glass make a candle with a lovely ocean view. Using the lay-and-turn technique, you can easily make wonderful theme candles with any kind of flat-edged embeds.

BEFORE YOU START

1. Select your container carefully. The opening at the top needs to be wide enough for you to get your hand inside so you can work on the sides of the glass. But the container should also not be too large. It takes a long time for the sides of a large container to cool, making it harder for the sea glass to stay in place.

2. Select your sea glass carefully, too. Sea glass usually comes in a bag with several colors of glass and a variety of sizes. Choose pieces that are somewhat similar in size and shape. Place them into piles according to color so they are easy to pick up when you are decorating the container. Don't use pieces of clear glass to decorate the sides because you don't want to have gaps in your color. Set them aside to use on the bottom of the container.

What You Need

Clear glass globe, such as a small goldfish bowl

Sea glass

Wick

Pan

Clip-on thermometer

Candle gel wax

Plate holder or dish rack

Bamboo skewer

Work one section of the container at a time, arranging the sea glass pieces from bottom to top.

What You Do

1. Attach the wick to the bottom of the glass container. Lay down a thin layer of clear sea glass on the bottom of the glass.

2. In a pan placed over low heat, melt enough gel to fill the container, heating the gel to the highest temperature recommended by the manufacturer. Use the thermometer to make sure the gel doesn't get too hot.

3. Gently pour the gel over the sea glass pieces on the bottom to seal them. Let the gel cool.

4. Place the container on its side on the plate holder. Arrange a few sea glass pieces against the inside wall from the bottom to top.

5. Reheat the remaining gel in the pan to its pouring temperature, and very gently pour a thin layer over the glass pieces on the wall. Let it cool.

6. Gently rotate the globe and repeat steps 4 and 5 until all the inside walls of the globe are covered with the sea glass. Let all the gel cool.

7. Wrap the top of the wick around the bamboo skewer placed across the top of the container. Pull it taut as the gel is cooling in the next step.

8. Reheat the gel remaining in the pan to the coolest pouring temperature. Use the thermometer to guide you. Fill the container with the cool gel, pouring gently so as not to melt the gel on the sides or disturb the arrangement of the glass pieces.

9. When the gel has cooled, remove the skewer and clip the wick.

DESIGN TIP

Once you've learned how to lay pieces of sea glass against the sides of a container, experiment with other dramatic visions, such as red, orange, and yellow pieces for a sunset theme, or multi-colored glass for a kaleidoscope effect.

Pin-Burst Candle

Colorful corsage pins make a striking candle. The trick to keeping all the pins in their jaunty positions is to first make a pin-burst gel core, and then center it into the candle container.

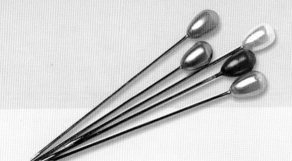

What You Need

2 glass containers:

1 cylinder to make the gel core that will hold the pins

1 candle container that is tall and wide enough to hold the pin-burst core

Corsage pins (or any other pin with colored heads)

Spray oil

Wick

Bamboo skewer

Candle gel wax

Pan

Clip-on thermometer

Metal spoon

Stick all the pins the same distance into the core so they look neat and orderly.

What You Do

1. Lay out your pins in piles according to color, and make sure you will be able to pick them up quickly.

2. Lightly spray the inside of the cylinder with the spray oil. This helps the gel to slide out.

3. Attach the wick to the bottom of the cylinder and curl it around the bamboo skewer placed across the top.

4. In a pan placed over low heat, melt enough gel to fill the cylinder, heating the gel to the highest temperature recommended by the manufacturer. Use the thermometer to make sure the gel doesn't get too hot. Pour the gel into the small cylinder.

5. Let the gel cool completely. Then refrigerate the container 10 to 15 minutes as another technique to make it easy to remove the core. (Don't refrigerate until the gel has cooled completely or you could risk too many bubbles forming.) Carefully pull out the skewer and then remove the core from the cylinder and place it on a clear flat surface.

6. Holding the cooled core in one hand, insert the pins into it with your other hand. Keep the pins pointing straight in toward the center at a 45° angle from top to bottom so they look like they are bursting out of the core.

7. When you've positioned all the pins, carefully place the pin-burst core into the larger container, making sure to keep the core securely in the center. Wrap the top of the wick around the bamboo skewer again.

8. Using the thermometer to guide you, heat enough gel to fill the container, letting the gel reach a temperature of no more than 200°F (93°C). (If you pour too hot, you risk melting the core and causing the pins to drop.) With the metal spoon, stir the gel gently, so that it all cools evenly. When the gel has reached the consistency of thin syrup, pour it gently into the large container, completely covering the central core. Make sure the core stays in the center.

9. While the gel is cooling, pull the wick slightly to keep it taut and straight. When the gel has cooled, remove the skewer and clip the wick.

Bamboo Prosperity Candle

Follow Feng Shui principles and light up your prosperity energy. The bamboo stays healthy in a container of water, surrounded by a gel pond filled with river stones and gold "abundance" rocks.

What You Need

Round shallow bowl with straight sides

Votive glass for the bamboo

Handful of unpolished river stones

Gold metallic paint

Prosperity affirmation stone

Handful of pretty gravel stones

2 or 3 stalks of bamboo

Mesh bag of polished river pebbles

Candle gel wax

Pan

Clip-on thermometer

Wick

DESIGN TIP

Using the same design techniques, you can make candles that hold any live plants, such as a "Good Health" candle that holds herbs, or a "Romance" candle with fresh roses.

What You Do

1. To make the abundance rocks, paint several unpolished stones with gold paint and let them dry.

2. Prepare the prosperity affirmation stone. If you buy a pre-made stone, fill in the letters and the symbol with white paint so you can see it easily. If you make your own prosperity stone, clearly paint the words and symbols on it.

3. Place a layer of gravel in the bottom of the votive glass. Fill it with water and put the bamboo stalks in it. Place it securely on the bottom of the shallow bowl near the edge.

4. From the bag of river stones, pull out the ones with shapes and colors that intrigue you. Remember that the gel will give the rocks a shiny sheen. Combine these stones with the gold rocks and the prosperity stone, and make an arrangement around the bamboo.

5. In a pan placed over low heat, melt enough gel to fill the container, heating the gel to the highest temperature recommended by the manufacturer. Use the thermometer to make sure the gel doesn't get too hot. Pour the gel over the stones to just below the rim of the bowl.

6. When the gel has cooled, insert the wick near the prosperity stone.

7. Each time you light the candle, say your abundance affirmations.

Fantastic Floaters

There's nothing shy about this centerpiece bowl with its fantastic floaters. In addition to looking absolutely wonderful, these candles will burn a long time without melting, so all you have to do is light them—and go party!

What You Need

Float holder made out of
a cardboard box (see instructions
below)

Utitity knife

Large plain glass punch bowl

Dogwood candle molds (found at art
supply or candle supply stores)

Candle gel wax

Gel dye, yellow, white, pink,
and any other colors of your choice

Metal spoon

Pan

Clip-on thermometer

Glass with a pointy bottom,
such as an old martini glass

Heat gun

Wick

MAKE A FLOAT HOLDER

Since the bases of the floaters are pointy, you'll need something to hold the floaters until you're ready to put them in the water. Turn a cardboard box upside down so that the flat sealed bottom is now on the top. With the utility knife, cut out circles in the cardboard to hold as many floaters as you'll be making. The circles should be wide enough to support the flower and allow the pointy base to hang in the clear below it.

What You Do

1. Place the dogwood mold on a flat surface.

2. In a pan placed over low heat, melt a small amount of gel, just enough to fill the center of the flower mold. Heat the gel to the highest temperature recommended by the manufacturer. Use the thermometer to make sure the gel doesn't get too hot. Add yellow dye to get a bright sunflower color, stirring with the metal spoon. Pour the gel carefully into the center of the mold and let it cool completely.

3. Following the directions as in step 2, heat enough gel to fill the petals of the mold as well as the pointy base you'll make in the next step. Add enough white dye to get a nice intense white color. Pour slowly to fill all the petals. Let the flower cool completely. When the flower mold is completely cooled, slip the flower out of the mold and set it nearby so you can pick it up quickly.

4. Meanwhile, make the base of the floater. Pour the remaining white gel into the martini glass, filling it up about two-thirds of the way. Let it cool completely. (See the how-to photos on page 92.)

5. Use the heat gun to melt the top of the base a tiny bit. Quickly place the flower on top of the base, pressing it down lightly if needed. The slight melting caused by the heat gun and the light pressure will be enough to meld the two pieces together. Insert the wick into the center of the flower. Remove the completely cooled floater a few minutes later and place it in the holder.

6. Repeat steps 1 through 5 for the other candles.

7. The candles will burn more slowly in the beginning and thus keep their shape a little better if you refrigerate them until you're ready to light them.

8. Pour the water into the bowl. The water level should be far enough below the rim so you can completely see the floating flower from the side of the bowl.

Make more floaters to fill small bowls and place them around the punchbowl centerpiece.

These candles will float and burn safely for at least 2 hours before you need to clip the wicks and re-light them.

There are three simple steps to make these long-lasting floaters. Use a mold to make the big gel flower shape. Then make the pointy gel base in a martini glass. After melting the base with the heat gun, slightly press the flower mold on top of it. The two pieces will quickly meld into one.

Design by Alice Donnelly

Color Swirl

In this distinctive candle, a dab of dye becomes a bold blue swirl. With the same technique you can make dynamic zigzags or graceful tendrils of color that seem to float in the sparkling clear gel.

What You Need

Tall container with a nice curve to it
Metal skewer
Candle gel wax
Clip-on thermometer
Pan
Gel dye, any color
Wick
Small bowl

What You Do

1. Place the metal skewer into the freezer.

2. In a pan placed over low heat, melt a little more gel than is enough to fill the container, heating the gel to the highest temperature recommended by the manufacturer. Use the thermometer to make sure the gel doesn't get too hot. Pour the gel into the container, leaving a small amount in the pan. Let the gel in the container cool just till it starts to solidify.

3. Place a few drops of dye into the small bowl. Dip the end of the cold metal skewer into the wam gel in the pan, then touch it to the dye. Shake off any excess dye and re-dip the skewer into the gel to seal the dye.

4. Stick the skewer into the container of gel and move it very slowly from top to bottom, creating a swirl of color. Since the metal skewer is still cool, the dye on it shouldn't melt before you reach the bottom of the container.

5. Place the candle into the refrigerator to cool it quickly so the swirling dye will not bleed out. When the candle is cool, dip the metal skewer into some hot gel to give it a quick coat and then make a hole in the center of the candle. Remove the skewer carefully and insert the wick in the hole.

Bold Perspective

Make this extraordinary candle by combining one bold glass container with a single, uniquely shaped embed. The secret to the combination is to use the distortion in perspective caused by the gel to help your design.

What You Need

Big, bold container

Bold embed that fits into the container

Candle gel wax

Pan

Clip-on thermometer

Wick

What You Do

1. Select your embed carefully. It needs to work with the color, size, and shape of the container; be able to rest safely and securely on the bottom of the container, and have a shape that would be enhanced by the distortion caused by the round container and the gel.

2. Place the embed in the container. (Since our embed was valuable, we didn't want to risk harm to it by glue-ing it to the bottom of the container, which would have made it difficult to remove later. But if it's okay to glue your embed, go ahead and do it.)

3. Although we decided that a layer at the bottom of the container would detract from the simplicity of the design, if your design would look good with a layer of glass beads or some other material on the bottom, do that now, too.

4. In a pan placed over low heat, melt enough gel to fill the container, heating the gel to the highest temperature recommended by the manufacturer. Use the thermometer to make sure the gel doesn't get too hot. Pour the gel carefully into the container, letting it gently overflow the embed.

5. Let the gel cool and insert a wick. Our embed was actually a candleholder, and thus empty in its center, so we just put the wick into the center of the embed.

Bonsai in Bold

This embed is a tiny tree made of copper wire and turquoise chips. We didn't know what effect perspective would have on it—and were thrilled when the tree's exotic shape and simple colors ended up fitting perfectly with the container's shape and green-striped rim.

Index

Acknowledgments
Many-layered and long-burning Thank Yous go to…

The wonderfully creative *Ultimate Gel Candle Book* team

Art Director Tom Metcalf, who captured rainbows for every page
Photographer Keith Wright, who made light do magic
Publishing Director Carol Taylor, who said "yes"

The vintage glass collectors who loaned us their treasures:

Elizabeth Bennett Cauley of Junction City, Ohio
Edna M. Kahl of Alton, Illinois

The companies who contributed supplies and expertise:

Yaley Enterprises (www.yaley.com)
Bitter Creek Candle Supply Inc. (www.candlesupply.com)
Deltcacraft (www.delta.com)

Gel Candle Designers

Julie Boisseau is a life-long crafter—a beadworker, floral arranger, decorative painter, and paraffin wax candlemaker. For the past four years she's also been a gel wax candlemaker. She's adding academic study to her practical art experience by working on her B.A. in Fine Arts at Western Carolina University. Julie lives with husband Ronald Boisseau and their three children, Tosanna, 17, Johnny Ray, 15, and Tiana, 7, in Dillsboro, North Carolina. Julie opened her candle shop, Flashy Apache Creations, in 2002. Visit her website at www.flashyapachecreations.com

Alice Donnelly began her creative career sewing and making fabric dolls and doll clothes. For 17 years she made paraffin wax candles, selling them at craft shows and at her candle shop in Asheville, North Carolina. Four years ago a candle supply rep introduced her to gel wax and she's been making gel candles ever since. Alice's gel candle design, Garden Bowl Potpourri, won the Best New Product award in the Body and Soul section of the Atlanta Trade Mart July 1998 show. Alice is the mother of two grown children and lives with her husband of 31 years, contractor Mike Donnelly, in Asheville. Visit her website at www.alcraft.com.